BELT UP!

A Brazilian Jiujitsu Guide to making the Grade

Gary Savage

Sav publishing

Copyright © 2025 Gary Savage

All rights reserved

The characters and events portrayed in this book are fictitious. Any similarity to real persons, living or dead, is coincidental and not intended by the author.

No part of this book may be reproduced, or stored in a retrieval system, or transmitted in any form or by any means, electronic, mechanical, photocopying, recording, or otherwise, without express written permission of the publisher.

ISBN- 9798273121782

Cover design by: Nick Bradbury
Library of Congress Control Number: 2018675309
Printed in the United States of America

*For Janet, thanks for your support and love.
And for John Boswell, gone but never forgotten.
See you on the other side brother x*

Thanks to Nick Bradbury for his great cover design.

CONTENTS

Title Page
Copyright
Dedication
Epigraph
Belt up   1
The Eternal White Belt!   3
Part 1   8
  The art of learning!   9
   16
empty your cup!   17
Leave Your Ego at the Door   20
Fight or flight   24
Part 2   29
Making the Grade   30
A way of life!   51
What a Cult!   56
age and the art   60
would Jiujitsu work in a phonebox?   65
  The Gracie's, the ultimate sales team!   70
Back to the future!   74
Part 3   84

Training smart!	89
The devil is in the detail!	93
the art of teaching!	102
Find a job you love and you will never work a day in your life!	108
confessions of an addict	111
conclusion	115
	116

BELT UP

A BRAZILIAN JIUJITSU GUIDE TO MAKING THE GRADE

By
Gary Savage

GARY SAVAGE

THE ETERNAL WHITE BELT!

'Success is stumbling from failure to failure with no loss of enthusiasm'-Churchill

Let's start with a brief synopsis of Brazilian jiujitsu. Brazilian Jiu-Jitsu (BJJ) is a martial art and combat sport that focuses on ground fighting and grappling techniques. Developed in Brazil in the early 20th century, BJJ has gained immense popularity worldwide for its effectiveness in self-defence and competition settings. With its emphasis on leverage, technique, and strategy, BJJ has become a staple in the training regimens of martial artists, law enforcement officers, and military personnel. The roots of Brazilian Jiu-Jitsu can be traced back to Japanese Judo and Jiu-Jitsu, which were brought to Brazil by Mitsuyo Maeda, a Japanese judoka and member of the Kodokan. Maeda, also known as Count Koma, travelled the world demonstrating his martial arts skills and eventually settled in Brazil, where he taught his techniques to a young man named Carlos Gracie. Carlos, along with his brothers, adapted and further developed these techniques to create what is now known as Brazilian Jiu-Jitsu. BJJ is unique in its focus on ground fighting, where practitioners seek to control and submit their opponents through a series of joint locks, chokes, and positional dominance. Unlike other martial arts that rely on striking and kicking, BJJ emphasizes the importance of technique and principles such as leverage to overcome larger and stronger opponents. This makes it an ideal martial art for self-defence situations where size and strength may not be enough to prevail. One of the key principles of Brazilian Jiu-Jitsu is the concept of "position before submission." This means that practitioners prioritize gaining and maintaining dominant positions over their opponents before attempting to secure a submission hold. By controlling the position and leverage of the fight, a BJJ practitioner can effectively neutralize their opponent's attacks and create opportunities to submit them. Another important aspect of BJJ is the emphasis on sparring, or "rolling," with training partners of varying skill levels. Through live training sessions, practitioners are able to test their techniques in a realistic and dynamic environment, allowing them to refine their skills and develop their timing and instincts. This hands-on approach to training is essential for mastering the complex techniques of Brazilian Jiu-Jitsu and preparing for competition. In addition to its effectiveness in self-defence, Brazilian Jiu-Jitsu has also become a popular sport with a thriving competition scene. BJJ tournaments are held around the world, attracting competitors of all ages and skill levels. These competitions are divided into weight classes and belt ranks, allowing practitioners to test their skills against opponents of similar size and experience. The belt ranking system in BJJ is a symbol of a practitioner's progress and skill level. Beginners start as white belts and progress through the ranks of blue, purple, brown, and finally black belt. Each belt rank signifies a higher level of proficiency and understanding of the art, with black belt being the benchmark in Brazilian Jiu-Jitsu skill. We will look at this in more depth later. Beyond the physical benefits of training in Brazilian Jiu-Jitsu, practitioners also experience mental and emotional growth through their practice. BJJ requires discipline, perseverance, and a willingness to push through challenges and setbacks. By overcoming these obstacles, practitioners develop confidence, resilience, and a sense of accomplishment that carries over into other areas of their lives. Brazilian Jiujitsu (BJJ) is, in relation to its derivative Martial Arts, still in its infancy. It has only been accessible outside of its place of origin since the 1990's, gaining worldwide exposure following the first Ultimate Fighting Challenge, (later to be Championship) in November 1993. The catalyst for this surge in interest was Royce Gracie (the winner of the first competition). Royce's family's interpretation of the Japanese Jujutsu and Judo that they had been taught, proved to be a puzzle that the predominantly stand-up combatants couldn't decipher. The elder siblings, Carlos and Royce's' Father, Helio Gracie, are credited with refining the techniques they had been taught and in their use of leverage over strength, in making the art more suited to the average person. In short you didn't need to be strong in order to apply the techniques that were apparent in the Japanese origin arts.

My Story

Fast forward to 2025, and Brazilian Jiujitsu is one of the most popular martial arts on the planet. My exposure to this art came after a life time of studying other martial arts systems. I was a Japanese Jujitsu Brown Belt when I first saw a grainy VHS of UFC 1. Like many, I thought that my style of combat was effective and had all of the answers. I had long been an advocate of pressure testing my art. My first book 'Does Karate work in a Phone Box' https://amzn.eu/d/26MjRHT describes my martial art background, the empirical research that I carried out, and how I came to study BJJ and MMA. Suffice to say, I discovered through many violent encounters on the doors and streets, that the techniques I thought of as effective would oft times prove to be as useful as a chocolate teapot. My frustration was compounded after witnessing Royce Gracie, bitch slapping and choking out these behemoth Martial Arts 'masters' with the relative ease of a skinny Brazilian taking candy from a baby. These were, after all, the halcyon days of the body builder. Those super freakish specimens that were all muscle, veins and mullets. The vast majority of the universe was brainwashed into equating muscle with fighting prowess. Royce and his family put pin to balloon in dispelling this ridiculous notion. They also de-mystified centuries old beliefs that oriental martial arts had secret and deadly applications. In reality the early UFC bouts resembled drunken bar room brawls rather than the balletic and precision-based skills that we had marvelled at on the silver screen. The Gracie strategy was simple, close the distance, clinch, takedown and finish the fight with a choke or submission hold. There were no lethal 'death blows' or 'no touch, chi knockouts' in their arsenal, but their efficiency and ease of movement was mesmerising. It certainly captured my imagination. From that first UFC, I became hooked on learning this system of combat. It wasn't going to be as straightforward as I thought. My second book 'All aboard the Gracie Train,' https://amzn.eu/d/4ACNO8u details this frustrating, and yet in some respects exciting and fun time in finding an authentic BJJ coach. Back in the day in the United Kingdom there were no blue belts in the art, let alone a Black belt. I went all out in my quest to become a BJJ black belt, but it would take the best part of 15 years, a lot of injuries, financial hardship and some wrong turns to see me achieve my goal. Today I am a 4th Degree BJJ blackbelt. I was amongst the first 30 recipients in the UK to be awarded the grade. My success in achieving the much-coveted black belt was not an easy one. As I have stated, it was a long journey from beginner to black belt with many pitfalls along the way. Some that were avoidable and some that were not. It is my intention to provide you with some insights, wisdom if you like, that I have accrued over time. Some things will be apparent and some not. I will delve into my vast experience of teaching and competing in this great art in order to offer some advice that may be beneficial in your journey and progress through the ranks. Just for clarity of the title of this introduction, I was a white belt for 5 years before I was awarded my blue belt. However, I mean the title of this introduction in its broader sense, in that we are all eternal students. We should always adopt that white belt mentality and be open to the art of learning. I hope you get something from this narrative. Keep on rolling until the belt turns black.

OSS. Gary Savage- 2025

PART 1

THE ART OF LEARNING!

An expert is just a beginner who refused to quit!

So, you have taken that first step and have joined a BJJ gym, or maybe you are considering Jiujitsu as a future endeavour. The following chapters are aimed at informing and guiding you through the early stages of your training. The white belt period of Jiujitsu is arguably the most important belt. You are exposed to a lot of information and concepts that will at first seem alien to you. I always liken the art of learning jiujitsu to learning the alphabet. At first, we have to recognise the sounds and shapes of each letter. As we progress, we are able to join up the letters in order to make simple words and phrases. Jiujitsu is its own language, you have to immerse yourself in it in order to understand it's meaning.
As a coach, it is my job to help you to navigate the alphabet, showing you how to put together your first words and form sentences that give flow. It is your job to take this information and write your own story.

The hardest part of your BJJ journey is already done, if you have walked through the door of your local academy. You have made a great decision.

Remember that there are no shortcuts in jiujitsu, you have to put the time and effort in. The hard yards, so to speak.

When I first started training, I always thought there must be some kind of Holy Grail. Something that only the Gracie family knew. A key that would unlock all of the family secrets and gain me access to jiujitsu Nirvana. If it exists I have yet to find it. I suspect strongly (through many years of seeking) that there is no Holy Grail. The key is simply hard work, tenacity and the ability to stay focused on your goal.

At Black belt I am still learning, developing my game and enjoying every minute of the process (an eternal white belt).

The art of Jiujitsu is ever evolving. It lives and it breathes.

I am very much 'old school' in my approach to Jiujitsu, does that mean I only use antiquated techniques? No, I will use anything that I like and can incorporate into my game. My mentality is 'old school', the way we trained and were taught, but I have an open mind and can embrace new ideas.

Comparing the jiujitsu of yesteryear to today is pointless though. We can learn from the old and new schools.

> *'The mind is like a parachute, it works best when open'*- Rickson Gracie

What to expect

Those coming from a traditional martial arts background may at first be surprised by the relaxed attitude found in a typical

BJJ gym. We show respect in our own unique way. Rather than bowing before a roll we slap hands and bump fists. In my gym before and after class we bow out and shake hands, but in terms of general rules, we are pretty lax, people will generally talk and laugh during training. There are no calling the Black belts Sensei etc, its usual to be known by our Christian names. Some use the term professor, but it's done in a light-hearted and fun way. Dress code is also very relaxed, we don't make our students wear our academy Gi, although I know that this happens in other gyms. My students are free to wear whatever colour Gi they want, although they should expect a bit of fun poked at them for a garish choice. At the end of the day, we are in the gym to improve our Jiujitsu. We are not a cult; we are a place that is open and friendly where all of the members are there to learn and get better at the art.

One size doesn't fit all

We also have to realise that people train for different reasons, some come to get fit and learn how to defend themselves, some want to compete and both are fine. Jiujitsu is for everyone, the hobbyist or the serious sport orientated student. I believe, intrinsically, that jiujitsu is first and foremost a self-defence art, but the sporting context is probably the most prevalent in modern jiujitsu academies. The new student often doesn't know what would be an effective technique for self-defence as opposed to the sporting application. It is important for the coach to highlight these differences. It is also advisable for the new student to ask questions regarding these differences. Remember there are no stupid questions. One thing that will be apparent to any new student is that Jiujitsu practice is probably 90% ground work. The traditional martial artist, from a striking background, may find this very much at odds with their understanding. It seems that it is acceptable in a lot of jiujitsu academies to totally ignore the takedown until well into a student's learning path. However, I think this issue isn't as prevalent as it once was. Modern jiujitsu is influenced, and incorporates wrestling, i.e. the jiujitsu student uses more explosive energy and that comes from a wrestling base. In addition, Jiujitsu coaches are seeing the importance of teaching takedowns, which is a great thing and to be encouraged. Judo is also a preferred choice for many as a great compliment to the ground fighting aspects of the art. If your academy doesn't offer a wrestling or Judo program, seek one out. It will pay dividends in your training, especially if your focus is on the competitive aspect of jiujitsu. At the start of your training, you may feel overwhelmed by the amount of new information and technical knowledge you need to absorb. It is not uncommon to hear new students say that they are struggling to sleep after training. This is a result of the brain trying to assimilate all of the new information and the adrenaline that is produced through the live training. It is a phase and will pass (in time). I recall lying awake for hours thinking about the many techniques I had learned, or going over my rolls and their outcomes (good and bad). Jiujitsu was in my head all the time, from the moment I woke till sleep eventually came.

It wasn't just my beauty sleep that was affected by my passion. My relationships suffered as a result of my obsessive training routine. I seemed in a perpetual ground hog day. Relationships would start fine, all sunshine and roses. My girlfriends even liked the fact that I was physically fit through my training regime. But the initial enthusiasm soon gave way to them feeling sidelined. I was, to be fair, training twice a day, travelling over 2 hours and even in my down time was consumed by reading about martial arts or thinking about it. Many of these failed romances, could have been avoided had I been willing to compromise. But I couldn't, or rather wouldn't. I was selfish and had tunnel vision. Oft times, after I was given the ultimatum ('it's me or jiujitsu') I felt hard done by. Obviously, I always chose jiujitsu, and subsequently hurt a lot of people (myself included) by making this choice. Today, in retrospect, I think that I would try to compromise a little more. I am lucky that I now have a partner who encourages me to go to the gym. She realises that it is good for my mental health, and therefore the quality of our relationship (either that or she just likes me out of the house).

I don't train as much as I did. But that is down to my health rather than desire. My left and right hips have been replaced and at 61 years young I can't train with the same intensity. If I could advise people to navigate training and relationships, I would say it is down to the individual. We are all on different paths. But don't lose the love of your life because you are incapable of compromise. You can have the balance of a relationship and training. I just never found a way of doing that in the early days, and always chose the true love of my life, Jiujitsu, above all others.

I realise that this narrative so far makes the pursuit of excellence in jiujitsu seem a cold and hard journey. You may be forgiven for thinking, 'hang on, this geezer has sustained two knackered hips and screwed up most of his relationships through training, I think I will swerve it and go to the pub (with my partner)'.

All true (the injuries etc). However, the benefits of training and learning jiujitsu, far outweigh any negative. Will it be easy, no. Will it be worth it, Hell yes. I should point out that my hips are a combination of the many years spent in MMA, kickboxing, Jiujitsu training and competing. Injuries and niggles are inevitable. In fact, if I awake pain free, I have obviously died in my sleep. I could have been a couch potato and still have physical issues at my age (different ones, but still debilitating).

These days, training is more scientific. We have access to better information and nutritional advice, which all contributes to healthier outcomes. Listen to your body, learn to rest when needed and remember that every round doesn't have to be 'to the death'. Take it at a pace that suits you. Enjoy the journey. Enjoy the training for as long as you can.

'Take care of your body, it's the only place you have to live' Jim Rohn

Jiujitsu is blind

You will meet a lot of different characters in a typical jiujitsu gym. The wannabe 'Mundial champion', the 'hobbyist', the 'obsessive' and a plethora of people that just enjoy the atmosphere of a jiujitsu gym. One thing that is apparent is that there is no prejudice of sexual orientation, race, job status or religious belief on the mats (or shouldn't be). In my gym we have every professional person you can think of, all training together with the common aim of getting better at jiujitsu (it must be like being in the Freemasons). The belt system is the only real distinguishing feature in a hierarchal sense. And this can cause some confusion for the new student. So how does the belt system work? The answer is probably different from academy to academy. Some grade from a syllabus and others measure progress through attendance and observing a student's technical advancement. It can typically take between 8 and 15 years to achieve the black belt. Which is a long time in todays faced paced world where people want things now, and with minimum effort. This is sometimes evidenced by the high dropout rate in jiujitsu. It has been documented that only 1% of people that start will make it to the grade of black belt in BJJ. Which means that although there are a lot of people that train, or have trained in the art, there are still relatively few black belts as opposed to other martial arts. So, if your goal is a quick white to black belt journey, maybe try another martial art. Anyway, enough of this infomercial for the gentle art of jiujitsu, let's get into the nuts and bolts. Sit down with a nice cup of something hot and refreshing and read on. But don't take the next chapter's title as an instruction and waste your brew!

EMPTY YOUR CUP!

'We cannot solve problems with the kind of thinking we employed when we came up with them'-Einstein

Let's start with analysing the statement made famous by Bruce Lee, 'empty your cup'. As someone brand new to BJJ you may well be forgiven for thinking that your cup is already empty. By cup, we are referring to your preconceived ideas, notions, experiences etc. We all carry around indoctrinated views as to how a 'thing' is, or should be. I recall thinking that this great new art was out of my depth of ability or understanding. That my body type (more Stan Lee than Bruce Lee) would never be flexible enough to apply the technical aspects required. It seemed to my preconceived, half full cup, that I would struggle to get into some of the more gymnastic type positions. And, whilst its true that my early attempts to invert or produce a similar shape that I was shown by my coach proved difficult, my perseverance and dogmatic attitude got me through some of my doubts and saw me eventually grasping the more physically demanding techniques. You may, like me, be coming to BJJ from another martial art. If so, there will be some 'unlearning' to do, but also some understanding of similarities that are apparent in all unarmed combat systems. Fighting arts rely on an ability to gauge distance, control space and create angles. Jiujitsu is no different in the importance it places on these principles.

Basic instincts

I am a firm believer that there are no 'basic techniques' but rather a set of 'basic principles' that once absorbed will make for a better understanding and ability to 'get' a new technique. We will delve into the core principles in a later chapter. When I started Jiujitsu, I too thought that an armbar was a 'basic'. I later understood that the 'basics' were more the high percentage techniques and this was why they are taught first. Take the hip escape. In most academies the first lesson you are taught is how to shrimp your body across a mat and told it is a 'hip escape'. Rarely in my opinion is the hip escape explained properly. I have a student, who came to me after taking some private lessons at another gym. He had become frustrated because the coach had made him feel that he was stupid for not remembering this 'simple' technique (after only two lessons). I asked the student to show me his progress and what he had actually learned. It was, as expected, the hip escape, moving across the mats in a line. After he had finished his demonstration, I asked him "what is the move for"? He paused for a while before admitting he had no idea other than it seemed like a good warm up exercise. I started his lesson by demonstrating how the hip escape is an important technique in creating space and to set up both sweeps, attacks and defensive strategies. I could see an immediate grasp of the technique, that 'lightbulb' moment that makes coaching so worthwhile. We used the hip escape to learn the scissor sweep, the kimura from close guard and as a way of escaping a tight side control. All of these techniques made sense once the principle of distance management and controlling space was properly explained. The hip escape drill across the mat no longer a 'good warm up routine', but rather an important principle. Remember, in life and in Jiujitsu there is rarely a silly question. If you don't understand something, ask. I often watch people on videos performing solo drills to warm up and wonder if they understand the application that the drill is mimicking or the principles that are being used. It is going to help you assimilate the technical aspects of a given move if you can visualise what you are doing in these solo drills. It is afterall BJJ's version of shadow boxing. You may be coming from a traditional martial art that has Kata (sequenced moves). I remember practicing Kata as a child. I had all the movements sharp and precise but to say that I understood what each movement was in terms of a practical application would be a lie. Karate teachers are now seeing the importance of the 'Bunkai' or rather the application of the individual techniques within the Kata. Solo drilling in Jiujitsu is mainly used in warm ups. In other martial arts solo practice is given a lot more emphasis. The other thing that separates BJJ from other (not all) martial arts is in the importance it places on 'aliveness', i.e. training in a way that isn't reliant on compliancy. Yes, we have to drill without resistance to learn the specific mechanics of the desired technique, but we also need to add some resistance through rolling (sparring) in order to get the correct timing and feel of a move. In traditional systems such as the stand-up striking systems we will often see 'dead patterns', i.e. total compliance, especially in the self defence demonstrations whereby you see the black belt doing 5 or six moves whilst the attacker stands statue still holding out their arm in a frozen punch. And, whilst there is nothing wrong (there actually is) with how people choose to practice, without sparring or live scenario training, all you will be doing is learning sequences that have no empirical value. In Jiujitsu we have a good balance of building the necessary motor skills with pressure testing. It is why so much emphasis is placed on rolling. It will take some getting used to, but this is where that most famous quote in jiujitsu comes into its own, 'leave the ego at the door.' Roll the next chapter.

LEAVE YOUR EGO AT THE DOOR

'When the ego dies, the soul awakes'- Gandhi

So, what do we mean by 'leave the ego at the door'? Well, this fits nicely with the previous chapter's advice to 'empty your cup'. Your preconceived notion that you are tough and know how to fight before you sample a BJJ lesson will hinder your progress, if not kill it completely. I have seen every 'hard man,' 'street fighter' 'I just see red bro' type walk into my gym over the years. Without exception by the end of that first lesson (if they make it that long) there is a shift in their attitude. I recall a local 'tough guy' come to train with me a few years ago. This guy could bench press a building. He had muscle on his muscles, you get the picture. His huge torso didn't adapt too well to some of the techniques we focused on that night but he got to grips (no pun intended) with it after some coaching. What I noticed, was that he was fighting every move, even though we were in the drilling phase of the training. I saw the frustration on the face of his training partner, and noticed a glint in muscle man's eye that said 'I knew it wouldn't work on me'. Now I could have made a bee line for this guy when it came to rolling, but I wanted him to learn a valuable lesson that night. I deliberately split him up from his training partner and asked one of my younger and more experienced lads to jump in with him. The young lad, Elliott was 16 years old, weighed about 9 stone and looked more choir boy than fighter. I stood back and observed as the big guy launched at Elliott. Elliott stayed composed, as he had been trained to do. He swept and mounted the tough guy, who at this time was flailing like a fish out of water. He was desperately trying to bench press the 9 stone Elliott off of him. Elliott held his position but allowed some slight disconnect which made the big guy roll onto his front. Elliott, sunk in a choke and tapped out the tough guy. It didn't register straight away and the big guy, obviously humiliated wanted to go again. Same result. He left the gym that night looking like someone had stolen his sweets. We never saw him again. Now to be fair, this was a roll in a sporting context, there was no punching or biting, eye gouging etc, but it proved a point, in that if you train properly and learn that being beaten is a part of learning in Jiujitsu then you will have a better chance of progressing. Now this can go both ways. Sometimes I will start my students standing up and allow striking etc. It is amazing how this changes their opinions of their abilities. If you want to progress, empty your cup and leave the ego at the door. Or better still just lose the ego altogether. You are there to learn. Learning will happen if you allow it to happen. You will have heard this statement a thousand times in a typical jiujitsu gym, 'there is no losing, only learning'. Every time you get tapped out by the overzealous blue belt take it as one of the best lessons you will ever receive. I remember as an (overzealous) blue belt, thinking I was the be all and end all because I was able (mostly) to tap the other students of my grade or below. I was like a shark circling, ready to take a big fuck off bite out of one of the unsuspecting white belts (cue the Jaws theme). A chance to notch up another win. Now, don't get me wrong I was never that 'blue belt'. You know the one, the self-styled 'mat enforcer'. I just loved to roll, and let's be honest we don't really hold back at the lower grades. This one time there was a visiting Purple Belt. Of course I wanted to roll with him, to test myself against a higher grade. Today it's a very common sight to see multiple purple, brown and even blackbelts in every session. Back then it was as rare a rocking horse shit. And to compound it, he was Brazilian. Now, here is the thing. A Brazilian doing Brazilian Jiujitsu was an enigma. It didn't matter to me that we were probably learning/practicing the same techniques. In my mind he must be leagues above me. I mean here I was, a gringo trying to wrap his head around this mystical 'new' art. In truth, even before we slapped hands I had lost the roll. My perception that he must have some secret ninja powers threw me completely off my 'A' game. Now to further add colour to this story, this lad was a good few years younger than me and outweighed me by a substantial amount. I realise it sounds like a litany of excuses and to be honest it is (ah that fickle mistress the Ego), but in all honesty it was a nightmare roll for me. I was handled with the relative ease of, well a cocky blue belt getting smashed by a huge Brazilian. The first part of my 'game' to be (easily) defeated was my guard. Now up to this point, I thought I had a good guard. I considered my guard to be my best weapon. A port from which I could launch a myriad of subs from. Well, this port was about to be compromised. In short, I was ragged around the mat like an empty jacket. After tapping out the rhythm to 'We will rock you' multiple times, I was left in a pool of my own sweat, staring up at the ceiling as the ghost of Ego's past, made an exit stage left. Maybe it was my imagination or maybe not, but I felt the burning gaze of my fellow students. I could hear the collective whisper of 'shit, we believed in you. You have thrown us all under the bus'. Of course this was all in my head. In reality, the whites and blues were busy scrambling like demented children in a game of musical chairs, to find an easy round rather than face the now 'king of the mat' purple belt. Bollocks, I realised that we two were now the only ones without a new partner to roll with. Round two (and three) went much the same way. I left training that night looking and feeling like I'd dropped the soap in the prison showers in front of Big Vern. The drive home felt like an eternity as I came to terms with the reality that I had been destroyed on the mats. Sleep didn't come easy that night. I went over the rolls in minute detail, analysing each and every position I lost, and each and every painful submission I found myself in. It was in hind sight a great lesson and an integral part of my development in Jiujitsu. I learned that night that we are sometimes the nail and sometimes the hammer. I also discovered that those white and blue belts that would do almost anything to avoid making eye contact and subsequently rolling with this guy would, in all likelihood, join the rest of the BJJ white and blue belts in the quitter's graveyard, never to feel the joy of levelling up to their next belt. They would either stop training all together or occasionally make a brief return before quitting again. For me, once the shock of being beaten so effortlessly had become a painful but distant memory, I was eager to go against this guy, or his equivalent, in order to measure my progress. I thank God for all the times I came up short. I hold dear the memories of those crushing defeats. I certainly learned some valuable lessons that would serve me well and help me to become a better jiujitsu practitioner. Fear not, or rather, fear, but use the fear to grow. It is rarely fear, rather adrenaline. You will either run into the fire or away from the fire. I'll let the next chapter explain my innate ramblings in more detail.

FIGHT OR FLIGHT

'The only thing we have to fear is fear itself'-Roosevelt

Many years ago, when I was studying Japanese jujitsu, (before anyone had heard the term Brazilian Jiujitsu in the UK) I was often overwhelmed with a sinking feeling every time I walked into the Dojo. It wasn't fear as such, more a feeling of not knowing what I was in for. To explain this in more detail, this was a rough old place to train. There were no easy spars. I was thrown into the mix straight away. I had to learn the hard way to keep my hands up or I'd eat a fist or foot for my lack of awareness. Fear and adrenaline are often mistaken. Adrenaline is the bodies way of protecting. Think in terms of flight or fight. The response of fight or flight is best summed up as our brain telling us we are in danger. It arms us to deal with whatever that danger is. For example, if faced with a salivating Lion, it is unwise to put your dukes up and prepare for a straightener. Our response, although probably one that would also lead to an unpleasant exit from this great adventure we call life, is to run faster than Linford Christie vying for an Olympic gold in the 100 metres dash. In more general terms think about a time you have been threatened by some neanderthal thug, shouting and gesticulating his/her intent to separate you from your head. You may well feel like you are physically scared, and this may well be the case, but your brain is preparing you for an attack. It will deaden your senses so that you won't feel immediate pain from a punch or whatever else Mr Neanderthal is using as a primary attack. If you choose to run (flight) you will be faster and more aware of your surroundings as a result of adrenaline. In short, your body is armed and your brain primed to give you the best chance of survival. Extreme examples I know, but you may well mistake adrenal response for fear when you are first entering a gym or even your first competition. Learn to harness this adrenal response. Jiujitsu gyms and MMA gyms have a reputation for being tough environments, but in my experience, you meet the best people in these places. The nail and the hammer AKA the white belt, may feel some intimidation when seeing the gap in abilities from the higher ranked students. Rolling is an integral part of developing the motor skills necessary in Jiujitsu. It can however be off putting for the new student to get absolutely annihilated by the upper belts. Picture the scene, the newly belted blue belts are all eagerly awaiting their 'roll' with the new blood. It is their chance to be the hammer after what seems like an eternity as the nail. They are excited to catch their prey in that anaconda choke they have been working on. They want to leave their mark, be noticed by the pack as 'one of the gang'. Even better, maybe coach will witness them easily beating the new guy and consider them ready to level up. Too many encountering this scenario in their first few sessions it can seem like bullying, or at the very least not conducive to their learning experience. Rarely is the intent from a higher belt bullying. They do to the white belt what they themselves experienced, i.e. 'learned behaviour'. In terms of it not being conducive to learning, it depends how it is interpreted. For me, I always took something from each crushing defeat. I learned quickly not to give an arm, or expose my neck. Remember, there is no losing only learning. Another thing that can put off a new student is if the techniques they are exposed to are too complicated for their understanding at that time. This can cause stress and add to the feeling of fear in being in the gym. Having all belts in a class is sometimes necessary, but the coach should try to have examples that are easily explained to the less experienced in the class. Fast isn't always best, as stated the dropout rate in BJJ is very high. This can be attributed to the aforementioned feelings of stress and trepidation. Other times it is something that is more to do with today's expectations. People want/demand quick results these days. Unfortunately, or fortunately, I believe jiujitsu isn't a fast learn. It takes time to understand the principles and to adapt to the physical demands. This is where you need to just enjoy the training, 'flow with the go', as Rickson advised. Every session will bring about some small, incremental improvement. These changes are oft times hard for the student to see. It is the coach's job to point out these improvements and to help the student navigate the feeling of not getting better and potentially quitting altogether. If this is you, speak to your coach, let him/her know how you are feeling. You will be surprised at how their perception differs from your own. Start to measure your initial progress in small ways, i.e. did you manage to escape side control, mount or half guard. Progress isn't always about how you subbed every one of your opponents. It is more to do with how you have defeated your negative thought process (and your ego). How you have made something that you thought was out of your realm of understanding work against an opponent in a roll. Maybe it is hitting a sweep, or almost catching a cross-collar choke. I recall as a fresh-faced white belt attending a seminar by Carley Gracie. He showed techniques that I now do almost in a state of not thinking when I roll. An example would be that old favourite of almost every beginner jiujitsu class, the scissor sweep. I recall driving home and my head spinning as to how obvious this move was, and yet I had never thought to use it. Carley had a way of teaching that looked so effortless. During my rolls following this epiphany I was sweeping all of my opponents with this simple yet effective technique. I felt like I should change my name by deed to Gary Gracie, such was my new found sense of improvement. In the kingdom of the blind the one-eyed man rules. I may not have known much, but I knew more than all my fellow trad jujitsu friends who hadn't attended the seminar. Anyhow, back to the idea that it is ok to feel out of your depth on the mats. The more you learn to harness adrenaline the better prepared you will be to handle things in general. The 'rolling' in jiujitsu is preparing you to handle this sense of what you are mistaking as fear. The more you do it the better acclimatized you will become.

'Fear doesn't stop death, it stops life' -Rickson Gracie

Fear, in and of itself, is a somewhat broad concept. We, as humans are scared from the moment we are born. We are programmed to be afraid, to not take chances, to stay on the path of least resistance. We go through the relevant stages of life tip toeing across a myriad of potentially hazardous situations and experiences. We are so fearful of the things that we don't understand, and in so doing may miss opportunities that could have been great had we only had the courage to take a risk. In essence our biggest fear, the ultimate unknown, is death. We will avoid the idea of our mortality at all costs. We dress death up in a big black veil, arm him with a scythe and refer to him as the 'Grim Reaper'. I mean, the guy is always off to a bad start with a moniker like that. We tell ourselves that death isn't the end, there has to be something else. The idea of a heaven, a place where we will be reunited with our loved ones, an eternal paradise, softens the blow somewhat and helps us to accept our fate. Fear of dying shouldn't stop you living and experiencing as much in your short time as is possible. Remember we are not meant to just exist. If all we are doing is following a routine of eat, sleep, repeat, we are already dead or at the very least dying. Jeez, I've depressed myself with that load of bunkum. Let's focus on some positives that make this wonderful life worth living. One of the greatest gifts that we have is our ability to learn new things. To grow beyond our perceived capabilities. Not so long ago the thought that man would walk on the surface of the moon was a dream so outlandish you could be burned at the stake for suggesting it possible. Or that we can be anywhere in the world within hours by hopping onto a metal bird. All of life's great discoveries were born out of someone's imagination and a lack of fear to try something that hadn't been attempted before. So, to bring it back to our subject matter, the Gracie family didn't invent jujitsu, but they dared to change its principles and applications, and further to pressure test that research in no holds barred fights. The great thinkers, innovators and pioneers paved the way so that we can move forward without risk. The fact is, that we are now living in a time of great technical and artistic advancement. We are all standing on the shoulders of giants.

PART 2

MAKING THE GRADE

'Strength and growth come only through continuous effort and struggle'-Napololeon Hill.

The Origins of the Belt System in Brazilian Jiu Jitsu.

One of the key aspects of BJJ is its belt system, which signifies a practitioner's level of skill and experience.The belt system in BJJ is based on the traditional Japanese martial arts ranking system, which was adopted and modified by the Gracie family. The grading system in BJJ consists of five main belts: white, blue, purple, brown, and black. Each belt represents a different level of skill and experience, with white being the lowest and black being the highest (other than the coral belt).The belt system in BJJ serves several purposes. First and foremost, it provides a clear and structured path for practitioners to progress through the ranks and improve their skills. Additionally, the belt system helps to establish a hierarchy within the BJJ community, with higher-ranked practitioners typically holding more authority and respect.

In order to advance through the belt system in BJJ, practitioners must demonstrate proficiency in a variety of techniques and skills. This typically involves attending regular classes, sparring with other practitioners, and competing in tournaments.

The White Belt

The white belt is the first belt that a practitioner receives in BJJ, and it signifies that they are a beginner with little to no experience in the art. The white belt is often referred to as the "beginner belt," and it is a symbol of the practitioner's commitment to learning and improving their skills. Practitioners who are white belt standard are typically required to attend regular classes and demonstrate a basic understanding of fundamental BJJ techniques. This may include learning how to break an opponent's posture, control their opponent's movements, and escape from various positions. In addition, white belt practitioners are also expected to show good sportsmanship, respect for their instructors and training partners, and a willingness to learn from their mistakes. The white belt is a time of exploration and discovery for practitioners, as they begin to learn the basic principles of BJJ and develop their own unique style of grappling. It is also a time of growth and development, as practitioners build a solid foundation of skills that will serve them well as they progress through the belt system.

Case Study 1 -Steve

Steve was a 27-year-old builder. His martial art experience was zero. He has watched the UFC since Tito Ortiz and Chuck Liddell traded insults and overhand rights. His main consideration for getting into Jiujitsu is to learn how to defend himself and his family if needed. He doesn't really want to go to an MMA class, but Jiujitsu seems like a good place to start. Steve, was a really attentive student from his very first lesson. He absorbed the techniques and, importantly, he tried them in the live rounds. His progress was fast. He was athletic and strong from his day job and seemed to assimilate the information well. His first classes looked at self-defence scenarios, punch defence to take down and control to finish. After a few months of training, my phone rang one evening, it was Steve. The conversation went something like this,

'Hey coach, I just need to tell you that this Jiujitsu stuff actually works'.

Me 'Erm I know mate, what has happened'?

'Well, this guy who is a bit of a bully started on me, he wanted a fight'.

'And' I ask ?

'I took him down with that double leg you showed me and choked him out'.

'Great, and did you get hurt'? I asked.

'No, he never touched me. But after I let him up, he wanted to go again, so I did exactly the same thing'.

'Great, see you in class on Monday'. I said before hanging up the phone.

NB Steve is now a Black belt and a beast on the mats

> *'Absorb what is useful, disregard the rest' Bruce Lee*

The White belt is all about developing and starting to understand the nuances of the art. In many respects the white belt is the most important belt in BJJ. There is an obvious emphasis on the white belt to develop a good defensive game. It is certainly a belt level that requires a robust defence, as all of the higher belts will be out to take a white belt 'scalp'. You are very much the nail and a lot of hammers are primed and waiting. The sharks are circling is an apt description.

One of the things I look out for as a coach is whether the white belt is engaged with the techniques. Are they actually coachable or easily distracted. The student at white belt needs to fully engage, to listen, watch and feel the techniques. I always think that the students that ask questions are most likely to progress, as long as they take the answers given and are not just paying lip service.

The time from white belt to blue is dependent on a few factors, i.e. how often the student is training, their ability to listen, learn and apply the techniques, and to a lesser but important degree their attitude. Attitude is both hindering and enabling. A good attitude will manifest as someone that is coachable and able to take instruction and critique well. A bad attitude will most certainly hold progress back and make for a bad atmosphere in the gym. Be respectful in the gym, be open to learning and engage with your peers. Above all don't be that white belt that starts coaching your training partners, when the likelihood is that you don't know the technique yourself.

White belt is the time for growth and enjoyment without putting too much pressure on yourself. Don't sweat the grading thing too much. Show up, listen, try and improve. The belts will come, so long as you continue to train.

There really are no short cuts in BJJ. If you want a black belt, check out your local McDojo where a bloke called Tristan (no offence to any Tristan's out there) is considered a 'Master' after 18 months. Remember, if it was easy, everyone (including Tristan) would be doing it. Wear your white belt with pride.

Prior to levelling up to the next belt, you may be awarded stripes on your white belt (1-4). The idea is to reward the white belt students' progress. I have witnessed some students of BJJ look disappointed to be awarded a stripe rather than a coloured belt. This is not the right attitude. A stripe in BJJ is a good milestone and denotes progress and a path towards the next belt level. There is quite a gap in skill between all of the belts in BJJ, so the stripe system is a bridge between these levels. Be proud of that first stripe on your white belt, it still signifies that your ability is probably greater than good old Tristan the Black belt in Mcdojo Do.

In reflection, the key to levelling up at this important stage is to be as present as you can in your training. Be that student that tries to implement the strategies and techniques into your game. Don't allow ego to hinder your progress. And above all else, understand that this is the level whereby you really get to understand defensive jiujitsu. Being the nail, is a phase that you have to go through. There is nothing wrong with being the beginner. We all started at the same point of reference.

It is also imperative that you show up and be consistent in your training. Aim for at least 2 x a week to begin with. Try to concentrate on the techniques you are shown in class rather than surfing YouTube for fancy techniques that you may think will give you the edge over your fellow students (they rarely do). Although there is no harm in looking at BJJ instructional material, try to pick your source wisely. Speak to your coach, fellow students (higher grades) about any good resources that you may benefit from. Videos can be a great way of going over a particular technique you may have forgotten between classes.

At the white belt level, it also will be of benefit to get some 121 training with your coach. This will help you to focus on your development plan and alleviate the risk of developing bad habits in your technique application. Get your 121 on video, so that you have a library of techniques that you can look back on.

Above all, enjoy the white belt phase, it really is a time of absorbing the essentials of jiujitsu, of developing the fundamentals and transitioning to the next phase in your development.

The Blue Belt

The blue belt is the second belt that a practitioner receives in BJJ, and it signifies that they have achieved a certain level of proficiency in the art. The blue belt is a symbol of the practitioner's dedication and hard work. Practitioners, who are awarded their blue belt, are typically required to demonstrate a solid understanding of fundamental BJJ techniques, as well as a willingness to learn and improve (no change from white to black). This may include mastering more advanced techniques, such as sweeps, submissions, and transitions, as well as developing a strategic approach to grappling. The blue belt is a time of refinement and consolidation for practitioners, as they continue to build on the skills and knowledge they acquired as white belts. It is also a time of challenge and growth, as practitioners are encouraged to push themselves outside of their comfort zones and explore new techniques and strategies. It is around this time that the rolling will be a little more co-ordinated, less thrashy and more controlled (I won't use the term Spazzy.... oh damn I did). It is also (or so it appears) the belt level that sees a lot of people quitting. I am not sure why that is, but it is likely a combination of the hard training and dedication required, and maybe some outside influences (work, family etc).

Case Study 2- Gareth

Gareth was a recently promoted Blue Belt. He was both strong and athletic and assimilated the techniques he had been exposed to easily. His rolling style was quite predictable, and yet could be hard to deal with. He really liked half guard and would flop into it at any opportunity. He had a couple of tried and tested sweeps that he favoured, and once on top he was a bit of a nightmare. During my rolls with Gareth, I would immediately shut down his movement forcing his back to the mat and taking away his hip movement. Half guard is effective when the person playing the technique can get to their side and work underhooks etc. Once flattened out the power of the guard is diminished and passing is relatively easy. I noticed that the lower belts were also working out the strategy and Gareth's game plan was foiled time and again. I could sense his growing frustration, and spoke to Gareth after class one night. I urged (recommended) that he change his approach, try other guards and in essence, leave his comfort zone. I also introduced him to the deep half guard as a way of transitioning into other options. Gareth, as expected loved the deep half guard but still seemed reluctant to try other guards or strategies. He initially had some success with his deep half guard, but it wasn't long before the other students got wise to his techniques and again started to shut him down. Although showing early promise, Gareth's lack of awareness hindered his progress and it was inevitable that he was soon falling behind in class. I am unsure as to why Gareth couldn't, or rather wouldn't, open his game up, but eventually he like many before disappeared into that phenomenon called the 'Blue Belt Bermuda triangle'. It can be hard for students to leave a comfort zone. They want to have success in rolling and as such they oft times stick to one or two tried and tested techniques. In my experience the best always try to implement new techniques into their rolling. They care little of getting tapped whilst learning the timing and correct application in the early stages. I watch them repeat the techniques until they start to 'own' the move, and it always makes me happy that they are able to 'leave the ego' and push their perceived limits beyond their current capability. In many respects then we may argue that the white and blue belt phases are the most important belts in BJJ. There are so many valuable lessons to learn and technical aspects to assimilate.

The Wolf in sheep clothing

Over time, I believe that the blue belt has changed somewhat. Back in the day, a blue belt was a God, as rare as Hen's teeth in the UK. Now, there are many blue belts and above. That's not to say that the criteria for reaching the grade should change, it is more to do with the logistics.
As stated earlier, the gap between belt levels in BJJ is wide, but from blue to purple is something of a canyon. I recall my coach Mario grading me to purple belt. It seemed surreal. I honestly felt unworthy. Imposter syndrome hit me harder than a Jake Paul right hook (joke). But seriously, I struggled to see how I had improved to warrant this uplift. I think back to my usual Saturday morning 121 with Mario at the Wolfslair. Usually, we would roll after my lesson, or he would ask one of the pro fighters who lived at the gym (usually a Brazilian) to roll with me. I started to feel more confident in my abilities in these rolls and even started to catch a few nice sweeps and subs. My growth was organic. I never really noticed it, but my coach did. I suppose I was validated a few months later when Mario and I, along with a few others from the 'Wolfy', went to Switzerland to compete in a European BJJ championship. It was my first outing wearing my purple belt. To compound my fears of being 'found out' as a fraud, I had to move into a younger age bracket. My first opponent was a purple belt from a Rickson Gracie affiliate school. Those niggling doubts were hollering in my ears as I stood opposite my opponent. 'You can't

win, you're just a blue belt wearing a purple belt', it screamed. And then something clicked as we gripped up. This Rickson Gracie guy didn't seem anything special, not even when I pulled guard and quickly transitioned to a triangle and finished with an armbar. When he tapped, I almost did a lap of honour around the auditorium. I felt like I had already won the Gold.

I did actually win the Gold that day after submitting my next three opponents. My confidence was at an all-time high and I realised that my level was right and that I deserved the grade that Mario had bestowed on me. Did I feel advanced in terms of my skills? Yes, to a degree. But it certainly took me a while to 'grow' into my new belt. I believe this was the case for every belt and I know that most people feel this way to.

In reflection, the blue belt is a great milestone in your BJJ journey. Be proud that you have achieved this level of competence. Don't let the ego act like quicksand, holding you down, unable to move on. Test yourself at the grade, but don't be too hard on yourself if things don't quite go to plan.

You may, at this stage want to compete or go to an open mat where you will be exposed to people from other gyms. Use the experience to reflect on things you have done well, and equally, things you feel may need work. Competing isn't for everyone though, so don't feel pressured into doing it because your fellow student, friends, are signing up to compete. There are other ways of testing your progress. Start by limiting your options when rolling. For example, work on areas that you feel need the most attention. It might be that you have a good guard, but the minute you are put in a bad position you panic and your brain goes to mush. In this example, actually allow your opponent to gain advantage and put you in a bad position. Start to analyse how you feel, what is it that is making you fail to implement the techniques that may help you to recover or sweep. Get comfortable in uncomfortable situations. Ask for feedback after your roll, i.e. what did you do, or not do that influenced the outcome of the scenario. This type of empirical research is so important for your development. Don't be afraid to admit that you may have a weakness in your game. This is the time to turn that perceived or actual weakness into a strength. The gym is, at this stage, your laboratory. A time for testing and making new discoveries. You can use the white belts students as your test specimen's when trying something new. It is a great way to develop your timing and applications. In turn, the white belts will benefit from you limiting your game. It will give them a chance to grow. Don't get hung up or feel any guilt in 'using' the lower belts as a way of you getting a technique down. We have all served our time as the gym 'lab rat'.

The Purple Belt

The purple belt is the third belt that a practitioner receives in BJJ, and it signifies that they have reached a competent level of skill and experience. Practitioners who are awarded their purple belt are typically required to demonstrate a high level of proficiency in a wide range of techniques and skills. This belt is indicative of the student starting to join the dots. The ability to link techniques and think in terms two or three moves ahead of their opponent.

Case Study 3- Gary

As I stated my purple belt experience was a mix of imposter syndrome and the high of winning a major European championship. If I am being totally honest, purple belt was my favourite grade. Maybe because I had great success. But also, I started to feel as though I really 'got' jiujitsu at last. The mythical art that I believed to exist, started to make (some) sense. It was also at purple belt that I first travelled to Brazil to train and compete. Of course, my expectation was still that we (gringos) were not really on a level playing field with our Brazilian friends. It was true that the Brazilian people had more exposure to the elite coaches and training partners. They also had more classes per day in which to train. Brazil was a real eye opener. We were exposed to some fantastic training and some very hard rounds. It was a shock to be training 2 or even 3 times a day, but it felt so good. The trip also dispelled the myth that a BJJ purple belt was better as a result of them being Brazilian. In fact, during some of the rolling I was shocked at how I was not only holding my own, but bettering my grade and above. The Brazil trip certainly put pin to balloon in changing my preconceived idea that we (gringos) were inferior to other nationalities that had a deeper history with the art. I came to the realisation that it was the training and effort that counted. Afterall, I had access to one of the best BJJ coaches in the world in Mario Sukata. I mean, yes, they had the sunshine, the beautiful beach life, the access to a jiujitsu academy on every street and a plethora of black belts, but what the Hell, we had………. Yeah, lets just leave that one there.

In reflection the purple belt is the grade where things really start to click. It is the grade that signifies you putting your stamp on the art. In other words, it is akin to taking the training wheels off the bike and that feeling of riding 'alone'. We all remember that joy as a child. The absolute freedom. The absolute feeling of pride and accomplishment. The purple belt is the equivalent of that feeling. The training wheels (stabilisers) have been removed. You start to develop your game. You are not so reliant on your coach (although you shouldn't think that you know it all yet).

Purple reign!

At purple belt you have probably been exposed to the majority of techniques that your coach has in his/her arsenal. Remember, it is at least 5 or 6 years of training to get to the purple belt. That is a lot of lessons. A lot of techniques. A lot of rolling.

A good, athletic purple belt, is a very hard roll. I have some absolute beasts that wear the grade. Their thirst for knowledge is reflected in how they look at all of the 'new' techniques. The stuff that maybe, the coach isn't particularly well versed in (in my case the leg locking systems that are very much in vogue at the moment). The purple belt is a highly respectable grade, but it shouldn't be seen as the end of learning, even though I stated earlier that at the grade, the student has been exposed to a lot of technical information. There are other aspects that are required in order to level up at this juncture. Your ability to learn at this grade has been demonstrated, but what isn't as obvious or indicative, is your actual understanding of the techniques. The nuances, the subtleties that often (always) lay beneath the surface of any given technique. That is not to say that at purple belt this exploration hasn't begun, it most certainly has (or should have), but not fully. At purple belt you are looking at the map, planning your route and have even brought a ticket to ride. The next step is to set off on a journey of discovery in jiujitsu. Not just the sporting, or even the self-defence aspects, but rather the 'hidden', or as Rickson describes, the 'invisible' jiujitsu. It is now time to realign your jiujitsu with that of being a martial artist.

In it for life!

Being a martial artist goes beyond that of technique. It is a way of life. A code by which we live and act. It isn't quantified by how many gold medals you have, or how many 'rolls' you come out on top. There is a world of difference between 'doing' martial arts and 'being' a martial artist. Of course, some people can practice a martial art for life and never be a martial artist. They are consumed with the physical and not so much the transcendental benefits. If your focus is purely on the physical aspect of jiujitsu then that is fine, but you are missing out on so much that a true understanding of a martial art can bring. As the great Bruce Lee said 'Don't concentrate on the finger, or you will miss all of the heavenly glory'. For me, I don't think that I was a true martial artist at purple belt. I concentrated on the finger rather than the heavens it pointed to. I was consumed by an ambition to win as much bling as I could, to be the baddest man in the gym. Purple belt, to me was purely an athletic achievement. I hadn't grasped the 'real' meaning of training. I hadn't started to look beyond the application of technique. My coach showed me a technique and I copied it and put it into my jiujitsu toolbox. A new way of winning a medal, of bettering my friends in the gym. I was obsessed with making the techniques I knew as smooth and aesthetically pleasing to the eye as possible.

Life begins at 40

It was around purple belt that Mario, my coach, offered some wise words. One Saturday morning after one of my

121 lessons, I had expressed some concern as to the fact that I was approaching, or rather had landed on planet 'middle age'. My question was about the decreasing level of ability that is somewhat inevitable as we grow older. Mario, although younger than me, spoke with the authority and knowledge of a true martial artist, "we have to adapt the techniques to allow them to work. We have to adapt our strategies in order to be effective'. Or words to that effect. It was around this time that I started to think more as a jiujitsu Ka, or rather a martial artist. These words resonated with me, and although I wasn't ready to totally put them into practice, they would underpin my understanding of jiujitsu and more importantly, martial arts going forward. In essence, the jiujitsu you favour to play in your 20's may well (will) look and feel totally different in your 40's, 50's etc. If you watch early footage of Helio Gracie fighting, his technique was very measured, but he was certainly more athletic (despite the Gracie narrative). His technical know-how didn't change as he aged, his focus did and his ability to perform certain techniques, likely did. You may (or may not) have seen the famous photograph of Helio performing a flying arm bar on his older brother Carlos. At this time the Gracie brothers were in their 40's. There is also some footage of Carlos doing some very athletic, almost gymnastic movements when he was well into his middle age. Great, if at 40 years old you can still move like you did in your 20's, but it should be practiced with caution and carries a risk to your physical well-being. I have never been able to do a flying arm bar, even at my peak. I just never thought the reward was worth the risk. Carlos Gracie was a great advocate of eating the right foods, stretching and introducing breathing techniques into his regime. These elements helped him to maintain enough suppleness to carry out the movements. My diet, on the other hand, was always more Greggs than Gracie. I was never particularly flexible, unable to do a box

splits (other than that one time when I slipped on some Ice, ouch), but I always tried to stretch before training, to some extent. My breathing technique has improved over time, slowing my breath to conserve energy, rather than panting like a demented sex pest making a nuisance phone call. Time and tide, they say, waits for no man (or woman). We all decline in physicality to some extent as we grow older. But that doesn't have to sound the death knell on your jiujitsu practice. Train smart for longevity. But also look to jiujitsu as a martial art. A way of living, improving and growing as a person. I will go into this in a later chapter. But for now, let's look at the next level in the BJJ belt system, the Brown belt.

The Brown Belt

The brown belt is the fourth belt that a practitioner receives in BJJ. Practitioners who are awarded their brown belt are typically required to demonstrate a high level of proficiency in all aspects of BJJ. The brown belt is a time to refine skill and knowledge and develop a unique style of grappling. It is also a time of reflection and introspection, as brown belt practitioners are encouraged to explore the deeper aspects of BJJ and develop a deeper understanding of themselves as martial artists.

Case Study 4- Hazel

Hazel had been training for over 15 years when I graded her to brown belt. Her response wasn't quite the one I was expecting (or maybe it was) when she called me a C***. Now for clarity, Hazel is more like a daughter to me than student. She had been through a lot in her life and I suppose I had a soft spot for her from the day she walked into my gym telling me she was going to be a 'cage fighter'. Many had written this enigmatic young lady off in her life, but I saw something beyond the rough diamond that she presented to the world. Her ambition to fight wasn't unrealistic. She was as tough as they came, trained with the sort of dedication I have rarely seen and had a fire in her belly. The fire wasn't to be the only thing in her belly and her pregnancy a short time later kind of signalled the end of her MMA ambitions. But MMA's loss was Jiujitsu's gain. She focused on her BJJ and was soon besting the guys in the rolls at training. As she went from brash white belt, to confident blue and then purple her life outside of the gym started to improve. She used her street smarts to open a number of successful business ventures, and in 2018 when I decided to move into a new premises and upscale my business, she asked if I needed a business partner. I knew that she was driven and savvy enough to bridge the (many) gaps in my business abilities. I could teach Jiujitsu and MMA, but I wasn't the best when it came to advertising, social media and moving my gym into the profitable and thriving business that it has become. Hazel was the perfect business partner. She has never been concerned with grades, and when she got her purple belt she cried, not with happiness, but annoyance, frustration or whatever was going through her head that was telling her that she should just stay at whatever belt she had. In reality, she would be happy at white belt. Purple belt wasn't too bad, as she loved the colour, but brown, forget it. For me, as her coach, she was more than ready to level up. I knew that she would kick off, and to be honest it was the thought of her reaction that I was looking forward to the most. As I made my declaration after class that she was being promoted, she bolted for the door yelling 'no, I don't want it'. Luckily, one of the lads grabbed her and physically held her in place whilst I tied the belt around her waist. As the cries of speech went around the gym (not something we usually encourage before black belt) I could see her anger rising. Her speech although short and sweet (C***) was followed by her hugging me and accepting that she now had to carry the grade. Hazel was, for the longest time, one of the only females in the gym. She was certainly the lightest person training and had (in her mind) a lot to prove. She wasn't able to muscle her way to victory in the rolling sessions. She had to develop a strong defence, a good guard and pinpoint accuracy in catching the blokes she rolled with. For a long time, she was the nail. But, over time and through each grade, her skills had developed. I eventually asked her to teach the children's classes. Something I didn't really enjoy. Her personality and the fact that her jiujitsu was as pure a reflection of what BJJ was all about (leverage over strength) translated perfectly to the kids. Teaching also really helped her to break down the techniques she had been taught over the course of the many years she had put into learning her craft

Brown Sugar

The brown belt is a great time of discovery. Not so much of new techniques, although that is still apparent, but rather as to how the techniques that the jiujitsu Ka has in their arsenal really work. It's all well and good knowing how to demonstrate an armbar for example, but knowing the mechanics and reactions that make the move efficient will move the student towards the role of teacher. Hazel has a unique way (even more so now she is a black belt) of explaining a technique by using her own made-up name for a move. It is not uncommon for a student to ask me to show them a Unicorn sweep, or an Ice cream scoop arm bar. Usually, my response, 'ah is this something Hazel has taught you'. I laugh about it and feign frustration that she makes up these ridiculous names, but actually some of them make sense when explaining the mechanics of the move (I never admit that). If you have made it to brown belt in BJJ you should be proud. It is quite an achievement. When I started it was said that only 1% of those starting BJJ made it to Black belt. I am sure that those odds are marginally better these days, due in the main to the wealth of academies and good instruction available. I still think it is a low percentage of people that make it, but 1%, maybe not. We still see a very high level of people quitting. And that is at every belt level. As I stated earlier, quitting was never an option for me. Since I graduated in 2011, I have in turn promoted a few black belts. Not really surprising as when I started teaching, I was a blue belt, so there were a few coming up behind me. I think from information I had, I was perhaps the 30th English born BJJ black belt, which given the number of UK black belts we have now is quite an achievement. In terms of female BJJ black belts, there are not a great deal to my knowledge in the UK. So, Hazel's achievement is very impressive also. It still doesn't excuse her for making up names for established techniques.

The Black Belt

The black belt signifies that the student has reached a pinnacle (not 'the' pinnacle) of skill and experience. The black belt is often referred to as the 'master belt'. Practitioners who are awarded their black belt are typically required to demonstrate a high level of proficiency in all aspects of BJJ, including technique, strategy, and mindset. This may include mastering advanced submissions, sweeps, and transitions, as well as developing a deep understanding of the philosophy and principles of BJJ. In addition, black belt practitioners are also expected to show leadership qualities, mentorship skills, and a commitment to helping others improve. The belt system in BJJ is a crucial component of the art, providing a clear and structured path for practitioners to progress through the ranks and improve their skills. Each belt represents a different level of skill and experience, with white being the lowest and black being the highest. By earning each belt, practitioners are able to track their progress, set goals for their training, and develop a deep understanding of the art of Brazilian Jiu Jitsu.

Case Study 5-Mark

Mark started training just after me. We have been close in grades all through our training. Mark, like myself, came from a traditional Martial Arts background, holding black belts in Aikido and Japanese Jujitsu. We always shared techniques as we were acquiring them. I would attend Mario's sessions in Widnes and bring them back to our informal little group in Blackpool, where we would dissect each move like mad scientists. It was great for both of us to have someone of similar ability to train with. Soon our little group started to grow and Tom from Preston joined our fledgeling group. Over the years I have watched both Mark and Tom develop their game to a high level. Both are now 3rd degree black belts. And yet, their styles differ quite a lot. This is where jiujitsu really shines. The art itself isn't a one size fits all art. Mark and I have a very similar game. We love the whole aspect of analysing techniques etc. I sometimes watch his teaching and hear him say something that I have said, or maybe I will use a phrase that he has said to me. Tom's game is also similar although he is very much a top pressure player. His passing is on another level. Mark will work methodically, slowly, in order to achieve his goal. Both are absolute beasts. Every black belt that I have graduated has their own identity, even though I have mainly been their teacher over the course of their development. It always fills me with pride to watch them 'grow' into the black belt. Teaching jiujitsu isn't for everyone (more on this aspect later), but I do believe that teaching makes your jiujitsu better. I have black belts who are phenomenal in competition who don't really aspire to teach yet, and that is fine. I certainly loved my competitive time in BJJ as much as I love teaching the art. One thing I truly believe, and that is that you never stop learning. I have learned from the world's best, to some lower belts that maybe have a great technique that they use. I am at an age now where I kind of missed the whole leg lock game. Having said that I have some great guys at my gym who are phenomenal leg lockers. But having had two hip replacements and being into my 61st year, I don't play their evil games. And there we have the grading system and my take on each grade. Please note we won't be going past the Black belt, as in the Coral belt, as I have no authority to talk about this lofty achievement.

GARY SAVAGE

A WAY OF LIFE!

'The purpose of art is washing the dust of daily life off our souls'-Picasso

Let's delve a little bit more into transitioning from hobbyist to martial artist.
If you are serious about jiujitsu and embrace it as a martial art that can offer so much more than just a physical pastime, then it can become a way of living your best life. Sounds a bit 'new age' when I say that, but in my case, it is true, and I believe that if you asked the majority of people that train, most would say that jiujitsu is more than a hobby. I used to feel somewhat insulted when people said things like 'oh its great that you have a hobby'. A hobby, in my mind is collecting stamps, train spotting, bird watching or line dancing, although people that are involved in these endeavours might see them as their 'way of life' (God forbid).
The fact is that jiujitsu offers more than a system of combat techniques. Once you are invested in jiujitsu it will embrace you tighter than a Boa Constrictor. It won't happen overnight, but rather it will creep up on you slowly. You might start to notice that you are developing an unhealthy interest in your class mates Gi's or rash guards. You will come over and run your hands over the material exclaiming 'wow, that is so soft'. You will find ways of justifying the purchase of new training apparel (what this old thing dear, I found it at the back of my wardrobe?). I often think that once you go to owning 3 or more Gi's, then you are well on the way to being completely brain washed into the 'way'.
 You will start to make that thumb and little finger 'surfy' gesture

at all times, I have even done it on wedding photos and once to my shame at a funeral. You will most certainly become a little more laid back and take on a bit of that hippy vibe (live and let live man). You might find yourself hugging your loved one in a way that Dan Gable (legendary Wrestler) would be proud. You might even start spooning your partner in a manner that would gain you 4 points in a jiujitsu competition. If these symptoms are familiar, it's too late, you are officially hooked on jiujitsu. There are warning signs that you have gone too far. The wearing of rash guards at all times (think John Danaher), or walking around Tesco on the 'big shop' in your Kimono, may be taking it a little bit too far in my opinion. There is nothing wrong with wanting a jiujitsu themed tattoo (I have one myself), but maybe don't cover your face and have the words 'Tap or Snap' on your forehead (it's not a good look).

But we see it so often that people adopt some, or all of the signs that they are 'all in', only to notice them slacking in training, not turning up as often and eventually quitting altogether. They offer the Gi's and other training apparel they have accrued for sale on eBay, trading their rash guards with jiujitsu insignia for whatever latest whim they get involved in. It is not uncommon to see an ex-student that you thought would stay the course, holding up the traffic on his/her carbon racing bike, adorned head to foot in Lycra. Until that interest dies and they move onto something else (probably porn addiction, or Devil worship). They most certainly are not what we call 'lifers'. A life sentence

The term lifer isn't just used to describe a serial killer. In Martial arts we call a 'lifer' someone who has dedicated their life to learning, improving and embracing the art or arts they study. They are people that are happy to serve this sentence without chance of parole.

Lifer's, look beyond the actual technical aspects of jiujitsu. They embrace a good diet and exercise routine that will benefit training. They can be spotted a mile off, carrying a copy of Rickson Gracie's 'Breathe", or 'All aboard the Gracie train (available on Amazon.... shameless plug).

The transition from BJJ 'hobbyist', to full blown 'lifer' is a sight to behold. I am not advocating being that guy or girl that is totally obsessed to the point that all other aspects of their life take a back seat. Believe me, that way is as unhealthy as not training. There is an argument for having balance in your life and jiujitsu, if practiced with intent and the right mindset, can give you that.

There really isn't anything wrong in buying several Gi's, in fact, if you are training a lot, they are a must. Buying books and learning all you can about the art you are studying is also a good thing. You should learn the history of jiujitsu. It is the same with watching technique video's, they can be beneficial to an extent. But, the main aspect of jiujitsu (or any martial art) is to 'participate', to learn and to continue learning. Sometimes the lessons are to be found by applying the principles to other aspects of your life. For example, it is horrible to be stuck under someone's side control. That feeling of utter helplessness. You can't breathe properly, and any mistakes that you make in trying to escape, will prove costly and most likely painful. You have to remain calm. You have to consider how every movement, no matter how small can help you to make the adjustments that may lead to escape. If you just accept the position and quit you will be defeated. If you apply the correct technique and principal you can move into a position that you can win from. Life is just like that. If you just accept whatever shit storm life serves you without fighting back, you are beaten. Nothing other than death is final. You always have a chance to make a small change in order to come out of a seemingly hopeless situation intact. Jiujitsu is a game of inches. You can 't make too much movement in bad situations. You need to control the space. Make incremental adjustments and believe in your training.

For me, jiujitsu helped me navigate a particularly bad time with my mental health. Having been diagnosed with Bipolar and having some serious episodes that saw me threatening myself and others I decided (or rather it was decided for me that I needed help). Of course, the first thing that most psychiatrists will say is 'you need medication'. They said it to me. They prescribed quetiapine, a typical response to bipolar to help with the psychotic episodes. I, like many, have been programmed to believe that medication is the only real way to treat disorders that affect us physically and mentally. I embraced the medication regime (for a while at least). What I was totally unprepared for was the effect that these medications would ultimately have on the quality of my life. I went from having energy and innovative thoughts, to being coshed and dull. I was unable to do the things that made me unique. I slept most of the day away and repeated that into the night. I couldn't train jiujitsu or concentrate my thoughts. I became fat (ter), lazy, unresponsive and didn't really care as to my personal life one way or the other. Yes, I hadn't tried to self-harm or threaten others, but only because I had no energy. I actually missed those days where I was hyper. They were (are) my most creative. Now, under this medicine, those heady days were just a distant memory. I started to realise that this bipolar had always been a part of me. And yes, I had struggled throughout my life. But, the one thing that was a constant, and kept me alive and (mostly) being a law-abiding citizen was my martial arts training. I hadn't needed medication all of the years prior to this, so why now. I felt as low as it is possible to feel. I knew it was because I wasn't training. So, there really was only one way to fight this, and it wasn't with medication. I decided (after a long while) to come off of the drug altogether. It wouldn't be easy; I was somewhat going along with the drug like a lemming walking towards a cliff edge.

Without Jiujitsu, and the other martial arts I had studied, I believe that my battle to come off the medication would have been a different story. I knew that through my training that nothing comes easy. We have to persevere in order to get to where we want to be. I also knew that I needed to understand the war I was about to wage. As Tsun Tzu said 'know thy enemy'. Martial arts have given me a strong will. I don't quit. I know how to strategize in order to gain an advantage and that is what I was able to do in order to get off of the medication and stay relatively healthy in my mind. I will add that if you have a condition like bipolar it is not advisable to do what I did. Seek medical advice and guidance before stopping medication. My approach worked for me; it doesn't work for everyone.

The upshot is that training in a martial art can teach you life lessons that will benefit you in all aspects of your life. You will gain wisdom, discipline and a strong will. All of the lessons you learn in jiujitsu et al are transferable skills that you can take with you as you navigate this great adventure, we call life

WHAT A CULT!

'Belonging has always been a fundamental driver of humankind'-Cheskey

Jiujitsu has been likened to belonging to a cult in recent times. The brain washing and ritualistic behaviour of some jiujitsu coaches has only added weight to this critique. It is certainly true that you come across some (right) cult(s) types in this great art. I have been lucky in that my lineage, through Mario Sukata, has always been supportive and none preachy. My philosophy on running a gym like a cult is this- It is unhealthy and doesn't foster a happy environment. Training should be fun, relaxed and informal (up to a point). Things have certainly changed from those halcyon days of dojo storming, challenge matches and fights on the beaches. Ah the good old days. We have had to move with the times, offer a more professional environment and cater for the needs of the majority. When I was first training and teaching (early 2000's), it was not uncommon to be challenged by people walking in off the street. They had seen the early UFC's and wanted to test jiujitsu's effectiveness. We never backed down and always obliged these inquisitive souls. It was good for us. We got to pressure test the effectiveness of our techniques. It wasn't rolling. These people didn't come to play fight, they threw wild haymaker punches, tried to kick your balls into your stomach and thought nothing of biting or eye gouging. In the best-case scenario's, I ended up with a new student after I had taken them down and applied a choke or arm lock. Other times the wannabe tough guy would leave the gym with his tail firmly between his legs never to be seen again. This sort of episode, although not happening every day, was good for the moral and camaraderie of the gym. It was a safe place to fight without fear of police involvement. My days of street fighting where behind me (at this time, I was studying Social Work and it had taken me over a year to be accepted onto the course following my previous convictions for violence, and I wasn't about to throw it away by going back to street fighting).

Another problem back in the (good) old days was loyalty. The Brazilian's have a term for people that don't show loyalty, Creonte. The word is associated with the legendary Carlson Gracie, and came from a TV show in Brazil, whereby a rather dubious character of low moral standing, was called Creonte. Carlson used the term against his former students, who had left to form a splinter team (Brazilian Top Team). Carlson would berate and heckle these ex-students whenever their paths crossed. This word and its context crossed over to other gyms and infiltrated the BJJ community. In the 90's in the UK, there really wasn't that many legit BJJ gyms about, and students tended to stay with their original teams (mostly). As the art grew in popularity and more and more gyms opened, people began to move around more. Today the term 'Creonte', doesn't seem to hold as much clout. People have been so used to the commercialism that is apparent in our Western society, that they think nothing of 'getting the best deal'. Now, there is an argument for commercialisation, in that it breeds good and healthy competition. People want the best training they can get and if that means jumping ship then that is what they do to get what they want. Personally, my approach is a bit old school, but I have definitely mellowed as I have matured. If people choose to leave my gym, then that is their decision. I get more annoyed if people leave my coach Mario (if that makes sense). I see it as disrespectful to the lineage where as I don't lose sleep over people that leave my gym. Thankfully it doesn't happen much.
Another aspect of the cult like behaviour in gyms, is in the forced

wearing of association Gi's, rash guards etc. We have our own club Gi, but we don't enforce our students to wear them. As long as a student is wearing an appropriate Gi, as in a BJJ or Judo Gi then all good. I don't really mind people wearing different coloured Gi's, although they need to take a bit of banter if it is a dodgy colour choice. Unlike more traditional arts we don't really go in for labels like sensei, professor or (God forbid) master. My students all call me by my first name or occasionally use the term coach. One thing we do, and I know a lot of BJJ gyms also do this, is bow out at the end of the session. I see this as showing respect to the origins of the art and your training partners.

Jiujitsu should be a fun and enjoyable thing. How you train is up to you and a good academy should cater for the needs of all of its students, whether hobbyist or wannabe world champion. But a final word of caution, beware of false prophets. These instructors will promise you the world but in reality, are unable to deliver. They really are only interested in your money. A better term maybe is 'false profiteers'. These types are usually interested in gaining a grade in Jiujitsu to add to their impressive list of Black belts in other disciplines. A way of making more money from their unsuspecting students. And whilst there is nothing wrong in studying and achieving grades in other Martial arts, these people are not interested in the art for art's sake. They just see a way to increase their student intake and add something new and exciting to their cult like McDojo academy. I know of one such instructor who was charging children an exuberant fee to grade to white belt in BJJ! Personally, I have never charged for any grade I have awarded, and certainly not a grade that you can mostly get free with your first BJJ Gi. It sounds ridiculous, but you should be asking questions about grading and fees before you sign up to any martial arts program.

You will be able to identify the lesser spotted McDojo guru by his impressive list of grades, his over use of the word OSSU, the number plate on his logo advertised wrapped van, SEN51E, and in some very sad cases his Steven Segal type pony tail and stretch wrangler (as worn by Chuck Norris) jeans.

OSSU! I'm not even sure what it means to be honest, other than as I have said, it appears to be the word most commonly used by your Steven Seagal wannabe's. These people are dangerous men (and women) who are capable of killing you with their little finger. They generally don't get involved in sporting competition because 'my art is street lethal, Ossu'. These masters are to be found, when not in the Dojo, bestowing the merits of a real ale in their local pub, or organising a good old session of Dungeons and Dragons with other like-minded 'Master's'. If you listen closely you may hear between OSSU's, how they were in the SAS (keep it to yourself) or at the very least trained the regiment in the art of unarmed combat. They have an extensive library of books and DVDs on the most lethal fighting arts. They worship at the altar of George Dillman and genuinely believe in his no touch knockout system of combat. The best of them once attended a seminar in Bury St Edmonds with the great man himself and witnessed his ability to render a double-glazing salesman called Roger unconcious by waving his hand in front of him, thus upsetting his KI.

AGE AND THE ART

'The best tunes are played on the oldest fiddles'- Emerson

I am a firm believer that jiujitsu is for everyone, regardless of size, age or any other excuse that people come up with for not taking up the art. I have had people calling me and saying such ridiculous things as 'I'm 40, is it too late, am I too old to start jiujitsu'? The answer is simple and wouldn't change if the person had said they were 80 years old. It is never too late and you are never too old. Yes, you will find it harder than the younger student in terms of your body's recovery and flexibility. But just because you are never going to do a flying armbar (or maybe you will), doesn't mean that you can't get great benefit from jiujitsu.

Injuries are the main reason that the 'older' student gives for quitting. It is not uncommon for knee, hip and shoulder issues to limit the progress and be a factor in the decision to stop training. We can't stop the ageing process. Time and tide, and all that guff is unfortunately a reality that we must all come to terms with. But and I believe this 100%, inactivity and accepting that you are 'over the hill,' will age you faster than training jiujitsu 3 x a week. As we age, we need purpose. We can't stagnate, we have to keep active and have goals in order to stave off the inevitable decline and official title 'old git'.

It is important that we 'older' grapplers, train smart. We know our own body better than anyone, so learn to listen to it and act accordingly. Remember, every roll doesn't have to mimic the final of the World championships. Roll smoothly and slowly. Don't get dragged into an ego battle with some snot nosed little cherub who is desperate to add your name to his/her list of kills on the mat. Just because the younger student has the energy and ability to 'explode' doesn't mean you can't better them in a roll. I have a student called Jason. He is a brown belt and not the youngest or biggest guy on the mats. But he has a good game, and can better a lot of the young guns by using solid fundamentals and tried and tested strategy. He embodies everything that jiujitsu is for me. He doesn't use his strength in place of correct technique, and he understands the principles that make the art so effective. He has had extensive knee surgery and other health issues that a lesser man would have used as an excuse to quit. He has adapted his game around these issues and continues to improve each week. I have heard him many times advising people that are his age or older that 'age is just a number'. His real strength is in his ability to believe in himself and not accept age or injury as a limiting factor, rather it is just another challenge. A part of the process.

The hips don't lie

As for me, I am the oldest on the mats at 61 years young (at time of writing). I have had two new hips and the thought of quitting repels me like a garlic clove to a vampire. After my first hip replacement I got very sick and ended up in hospital with a nasty infection that was life threatening. I was forced away from jiujitsu for several months, whilst my body healed both from the hip operation and the infection. But, being forced to stop wasn't on my agenda. I used the time as soon as I was able, to plan my return. I was like a demented mad scientist, coming up with ways to not only continue training, but to improve and evolve. I started thinking about every position in jiujitsu and if there were tweaks, I could make to improve my chances in their application. I was running scenarios like I was watching a giant movie screen of the rolls I would have, or certain techniques I wanted to improve. I think in hind sight the morphine I was taking was acting as a muse. I could clearly see each nuance and feel where I needed my weight distribution in order to maximise my functionality.

I have read a lot of books on mental preparation during my competitive years and knew that even though I couldn't physically do a technique, I could envisage it and practice it in my mind (again I give thanks to the morphine). When I eventually returned and was able to test my theories in actual practice, I was amazed how well they worked. I had really looked at my half guard game during the morphine period. I knew that I would struggle to hold or use that position given that I had a new hip, and the other was in dire need of surgery. The concept I imagined, and had practiced hundreds of times in my mind, worked so well that my students started asking me to teach my application. My second hip surgery was a breeze and even though it was only 8 weeks ago (at time of writing) I am back on the mats and even rolling with some caution. The point is, we do not have to accept something major like a hip, or in my case, double hip replacement as a death knell to our time on the mats.

We should always be looking at techniques and where applicable adapt/improve them.

As we age, we need to change our technique to suit any physical limitations we may have. If you are training and applying techniques in your late 40's and beyond that you used in your 20's I would be very surprised. The changes may be minute, but they will be apparent. Think in a broader term how your day-to-day life has changed. In my 20's I was running 5 miles a day. These days I would struggle to run for a bus. I could still catch the bus (probably) but I know that those times I miss the bus, another will come along and I just need to be patient and arrive at my destination a little later than planned. I am speaking hypothetically in order to make my point. In truth I haven't been on a bus for a good few year. I found that other forms of transport suited me better. This is jiujitsu. You will find ways to achieve your goal, reach your destination in a different way. Some way that suits your body and is less sprint and more measured.

 The story of the Turtle and the Hare, exemplifies the narrative better than anything. Speed for speeds sake isn't always the best strategy in getting to your destination in the most efficient way. Sometimes, I watch my younger and more athletic students moving like whirling dervish's. But, moving for moving's sake, isn't as effective as taking your time and establishing strong positional dominance. In the style of Jiujitsu that I am lucky to have studied under Mario Sukata, emphasis has always been placed on making your positions count. Your side control, for example should be very uncomfortable for your opponent. Your guard pass should almost take their soul. There is of course a time and benefit to fast and explosive movement. But this style has a sell by date. You should consider how your technique will look when your body has inevitably declined. This is a true and effective representation of the art. Adapting the techniques that you have been taught is not disrespectful, it is evolutionary. Had our teachers and their teachers not adapted techniques, we would all be studying Judo.

 The jiujitsu of Helio and Carlos Gracie bears little resemblance to that of Gordon Ryan in its movement to the goal of submission. It is only the end result, i.e. the submissions that are recognisable. After all an armbar is an arm bar, right? (maybe). As the art has evolved so too has the need for more intricate ways to pass the guard, sweep and control. That is a fact. And no matter what side of the fence you sit on, Gracie Jiujitsu as a predominantly self defence system or the more popular incarnation that we see in its sporting guise, there are changes within each to move with the times. Whether you like it or not, as the prophet Bob Dylon predicted, 'the times they are a changin'. Only the core principles remain the same.

'Adapt or be destroyed' Bruce Lee

WOULD JIUJITSU WORK IN A PHONEBOX?

'If you want to learn to swim, jump into the water. On dry land, no frame of mind is ever going to help you'-Bruce Lee

Bizarre title for a chapter? Let me explain. My first book, 'Does Karate Work in a phone box', pissed off a lot of wannabe Mr Miyagi's. I went on a number of podcasts and faced a lot of backlash over the title. I had random Karate 'Masters', messaging me to say yes karate would work, what about headbutts, eye gouging, elbow strikes etc? Everyone missed the point of the title. Not one of these people had taken to look beyond the title. As they say, you should never judge a book by its cover.

The narrative of DKWIAPB was more to do with the limitations we have in life, whether that be physical or mental. Those that took the time to read the book, discovered that it isn't just a book about using martial arts in a street fighting scenario. Although there are countless stories detailing violent encounters. intrinsically, the book is a celebration of the power of a martial art. The benefits it bestows beyond the physical. But I make no apology for asking the question, how effective is karate or for that matter jiujitsu as a self defence system?

Of course, every combat system has merit. But taken out of its typical arena, is it a 'be all and end all' self defence system?

'Karate doesn't work in a phone box'- Billy Savage

I started learning unarmed combat systems from a very young age. I was fortunate that my late father had been an unarmed combat instructor in the British Army. He taught me to box, to use elbows, knees and some joint manipulation techniques. He taught me the importance of hitting first and hitting hard. He questioned my decision to join a Karate school at 12 years old. He would watch me perform my kata and various techniques that I had been taught in class with a wry old glint in his eye. I was, like many in the 70's, obsessed with all things Bruce Lee. This was way before we realised that Lee was all for simplicity of technique and didn't advocate the high kicks and as my dad called the 'flowery' techniques, that his movies were chock full of. I recall sitting in our family car and asking my dad, 'what is the best fighting system' or something along those lines. His response was to use anything that was practical. He went on to say 'Karate is ok, but it wouldn't be as effective in small and confined areas'. I didn't understand and pressed him to elaborate. 'Well, put it this way, Karate wouldn't work in a phone box. There is no room for the kicks and punches, it would have to adapt to the small space'. As much as his answer pissed me off, I had to agree that such a scenario would limit the options available. This conversation, although seemingly unimportant, started an obsessive search for the 'truth'. I had a great friend in school who was into Judo. We would lament for hours the practicality of our respective arts (probably the reason why I left school with only a couple of O levels). It was the age-old Grappler vs Striker debate. We would spar endlessly, he trying to take me down with a throw, me trying to land the perfect kick or punch. Our empirical research was never conclusive. I suppose we were not at a level of skill to represent our arts to their best. What it did for me personally, was to open my mind to the idea that there were situations that demanded space and some that were more effective in close proximity. Just as my dad had tried to explain with his 'Karate Doesn't work in a phone box' analogy.

I started to question my Karate training and look to a system that seemed to have both striking and grappling within its arsenal, Jujitsu. I was convinced that at 13 years old I had found the best system of self-defence. I was of course blinkered to the fact that a lot of the techniques that seemed so effortless, were amplified by compliancy. And further, that the techniques that looked so cool, were formulated in the time of feudal Japan. The relevance being that the techniques worked as a result of the Samurai being clad in heavy armour, thus making it easier to block and catch a would-be attacker thrusting a knife or club in a downward motion at your head. It also later became apparent that in all of the times I thought about someone knifing you, why would they not just thrust it into your stomach or chest in a straight line, rather than arcing it down towards the top of your head. Jeez, I just realised I'm going to get another shed load of Jujutsu experts telling me that I am talking rubbish and that this attack is relatively common. Yes, in the days of the Samurai it maybe was, but not on the streets of the UK in the 21st century.

The point is this. Every Martial Art has its techniques that were formulated a good few hundred if not thousands of years ago. Unless, that is, the fighting system is something new, like oh I don't know, let's say Brazilian Jiujitsu. Now that couldn't possibly have any techniques that were useful against a Samurai wielding a sword or knife, or could it? There really is nothing new under the sun. Brazilian Jiujitsu in its self-defence application leans heavily towards its ancestor, Japanese Jujitsu, which as we have seen was developed to add to the fighting systems as practiced by the Samurai. They needed an answer for when they had lost their sword in the heat of battle.

Brazilian Jiu-jitsu is effective due to its aliveness as stated in other chapters. In other words, it doesn't just rely on unrealistic techniques that if applied against a resisting opponent would fall down faster than a one-legged man in an arse kicking contest.

Does it have all the answers in a self-defence scenario if such a thing exists? The answer is an emphatic no. I don't believe that any self defence system has all the answers, I mean I have yet to see an effective defence against a gun.

The problem with self-defence training is that it is impossible to simulate a real threat scenario. In other words, I am sure that Roger, an accountant (not an instruction), from Hemel Hempstead, is more than capable of disarming Colin, an IT worker, of a plastic knife that is lunged at half speed towards his middle-aged paunch. Now, take our mate Roger and put him in an alleyway (it is always an alleyway) at night, and see how he applies these techniques against a desperate junkie demanding his wallet. I don't know, but I am pretty certain that if Roger tries to take the knife in the way that his martial arts coach has convinced him is practical, then the next time we hear of Roger is in the local obituary column.

Some of the absolute tosh that is being peddled as 'real self-defence' is quite frankly, dangerous to the person being taught it. Brazilian Jiu-jitsu falls down (pun intended) against multiple attackers, as do most systems. It is unwise to be rolling about on the floor against multiple attackers who are intent on stamping their boot print into your head, whilst you apply a perfect triangle choke on their mate.

BJJ is a great system against a one-on-one threat, whereby no weapons are being used. Taking a fight to the ground, or this happening as a result of circumstance is in the arts wheelhouse. It is great for controlling a situation without the need of excessive strikes etc. And whilst this is all good, it doesn't, in its sporting guise practice striking techniques. Jiujitsu is best practiced with a good striking art such as boxing or Muay Thai in order to negate its weakness in this area.

The fox and the cat

Cross training in different systems gained popularity in the late 80's. And although it is still regarded as a great idea in terms of self-defence, techniques used, need to be practical and easy to remember. It is no use knowing 100 ways to take someone to the ground if you are not completely confident in any one of the hundred options. Too many techniques will only prove cumbersome and make your decision making slow in a live situation. It reminds me of the fable of the fox and the cat. The Fox boasted that he knew 1000 ways to escape the pack of dogs, the cat only had one. On the day that the pack came for the pair, the fox was caught as he tried to decide which one of his 1000 ways to escape to use. The cat watched from the tree he had climbed. Don't be the fox. A good right cross, drilled to the point whereby it is instinctive will serve you well, as will a solid takedown. As Bruce Lee said 'I don't fear the man that practices 1000 techniques, I fear the man that practices a technique 1000 times or words to that effect, you get the gist.

A robust self defence system is akin to a Swiss army knife, it can adapt and has tools for a multitude of situations.

THE GRACIE'S, THE ULTIMATE SALES TEAM!

'I have a dream'- Martin Luther King

November 12th 1993, the Ultimate Fighting Championship or Challenge, as it was originally called, was held in Denver, Colorado. We now know that the competition, the brainchild of Rorian Gracie and Art Tatum, would revolutionise the Martial Arts world.

Rorian Gracie knew that this was the perfect launch pad for his family's art. He also knew that the odds were heavily stacked in the Gracie's favour. Afterall, the family had been carrying out empirical research in their challenge matches against other Martial Arts for many years prior to the UFC's inception.

In essence, the UFC was nothing if it wasn't an infomercial, promoting Brazilian Jiujitsu to the world. It was genius in terms of a marketing strategy. The Martial Arts community really brought into the Gracie ideology. Overnight, or at least very soon after the first UFC, Jiujitsu, or rather Gracie Jiujitsu, became the most sought after, must have, Martial Art accessory to have.

Everyone, it seemed was bored of Kung-Fu fighting and wanted to learn to Grapple like Royce.

Rorian, chose the least aggressive looking member of the family to represent. He knew that had he chose a family member who looked jacked and sporting a face that looked like it had been smacked with a baseball bat, no one would buy into the dream.
The dream was that Gracie Jiujitsu was developed for the everyman. It didn't matter that you be old, weak, small etc. The arts USP (unique selling point) was that if you used the magic of 'leverage', you could come out on top. And it worked. By using Royce, the fresh faced, unassuming younger brother, the art could be best showcased. Now, throw into the mix the other competitors and you had the ultimate proving ground.
It is fair to assume that the other Martial Artist's competing on that first show, had no, or little idea, what they were getting into. The array of arts represented was fair. But in essence each was merely cannon fodder for the Gracie onslaught that was about to happen.
Each combatant, that stepped into the octagon opposite Royce Gracie, was served a harsh and painful lesson in reality. The Gracie family knew how each fight would play out. They knew that in the main, the competition was wholly unprepared to fight on the ground. With the exception of Ken Shamrock, the other combatants, were mainly versed in traditional stand-up arts. Even the inclusion of Shamrock was calculated. Ken Shamrock was a shoot fighter. A relative newcomer in combat sports. (shoot fighting, not Shamrock) Shamrock was also jacked, an all-American athlete who had competed in Japan. The fight between Gracie and Shamrock was always the big story of UFC 1.

The world loves a good underdog story. Think Rocky Balboa. Royce was Balboa. Fighting against the odds. His victory reinforced the narrative that good can overcome evil, small can topple the giant, much like a David and Goliath scenario.
By the time Royce was holding aloft a giant cheque and talking about a trip to Disneyland, his and his family's legacy was cemented. The Gracie train had arrived and everyone wanted to get aboard. Rorian, the genius behind the UFC, was quick

to capitalise. Soon after the inaugural competition, he released a series of VHS tapes, showcasing and teaching the 'basics' of the art. In addition, a series of pre-UFC challenge matches were released called 'Gracie in action'. Again, a marketing phenomenon, designed to introduce the rest of this fighting dynasty. Soon the world was clamouring to learn about Helio, Rickson et al. The Gracie family built an empire, through blood sweat and more than likely, the occasional tear. They had solidified their place in Martial Arts history and created an almost mythical legacy amongst their peers.

Whether Rorian was a master of PR, or just a very proud member of this dynasty of fighters, is in retrospect unimportant. Whatever the motivation, the Gracie contribution to modern day combative systems, far outweighs any bias or claims of manipulation that are often voiced by those too lost in their own bubble to objectively make.

Of course, the old guard, traditional Martial artists, would deny the evidence that BJJ was, at least in these early UFC matches, the most efficient.

Rorian did what he set out to do, he proved his family's art on the most brutal stage of all. These bare knuckle, minimum rule fights, showcased BJJ in all of its barbaric and beautiful glory. The Martial Kingdom heralded a call to arms. A fresh Prince had entered the courtyard. In Martial Art folklore, this was the ultimate fairytale.

Now, some 30 years later, BJJ is still revered as one of the most efficient forms of hand-to-hand combat, and probably the reason you are reading this tome. To say that it has changed somewhat from that early introduction in 1993 is an absolute understatement. However, comparing the jiujitsu of yesterday to today is a pointless endeavour. The BJJ of those early UFC matches was of its time. It had little resistance from the predominately well-versed stand-up fighters. These days, the natural evolution has seen the art adapt in ways that make it seem like it isn't as important in the many facets that now make up MMA. Changes are often born out of necessity and with the creation of MMA, with its inference on being as complete a fighter as possible, the ground fighting aspects of BJJ are arguably an area that has been relegated in terms of its importance.

But what of the future of our beloved art, the Gracie family sold us a dream, but has it turned out as we expected?

BACK TO THE FUTURE!

'Roads? Where we're going, we don't need roads' -Doc Brown

Where are we now, some 30 years after UFC 1? What is our Delorian time machine going to reveal? The question of the here and now and the future outlook is something I have often pondered. Those of us (old gits) that have been involved in BJJ since the early days, have seen many significant changes. And whether you are sitting on the 'change is good' or 'change is bad' fence, is not really relevant. Change is inevitable.

In terms of how much BJJ has evolved (changed) since Royce Gracie shocked the world at UFC 1, you could say significantly. The art in its role as a component of MMA has been downgraded as we heard in the previous chapter. These days the percentage of fights that are determined by submission is markedly lower than knockouts or decision wins. This is twofold. The combatants are savvy to the techniques that a BJJ practitioner has in their tool bag. They also train in the art and that arms them with more than just the ability to submit their opponent. They are skilled at staying safe. The second variable, is that the rules are different now. 3 x 5-minute rounds (unless a championship belt), doesn't afford a jiujitsu practitioner a great deal of time to implement their submission strategy. There is arguably a third aspect. The general lack of understanding (still) by the viewing public. They are more inclined to boo the fighters if the fight goes to ground. And although it shouldn't sway a decision to stand the fighters back up, we have to wonder.

Back in the day, the lack of rules, i.e. weight divisions, no gloves, combatants wearing Gi's etc, and the ground fighting being the 'new kid on the block', there were more chances of a submission outcome.

But, even with the rule changes and the other factors presented, Jiujitsu is still an essential aspect of the melting pot that is MMA. The ability to control and implement strikes, the essential skill of defending from the back etc, keeps it relevant and actually, makes it more likely to contribute to the final outcome of a fight.

Jiujitsu, in its true identity is a self-defence art. Let's look at its evolution away from the MMA scene. When I first started to train it was the Gi aspect that was most popular. In fact, it is common for people (of a certain age and experience) to say that BJJ is only Gi related and anything else is submission wrestling (more on this later). For now, let's look at the self-defence aspect and how the way we train may have changed over the years. As I have stated and written about (Does Karate work in a phone box), my reasons for training in martial arts was always about its authenticity in a live situation. I was fighting more than was healthy, and needed a system of unarmed combat that was 'fit for purpose'. UFC 1 opened my, and many eyes, as to the need to add a grappling based system to our striking skills. BJJ was a revolutionary art. It shone a spotlight on the aspects of real, ugly and violent confrontations. The Gracie family purported that 90% of all violent encounters would end up on the ground. And it must be stated that my own empirical research had shown that this may be a valid theory.

The early VHS tapes, released by Rorian Gracie were focused mainly (if not exclusively) on the self-defence techniques that are a major part of the Gracie Jiujitsu syllabus. Don't forget, this was way before there were any BJJ coaches in the UK. We had to take whatever crumb was offered. I had every tape and watched and studied them religiously. Some of the techniques looked almost exactly like those I had learned from my dad, and in my traditional jujitsu classes. And some didn't. Had Rorian Gracie advocated that I learn the Argentinian Tango as part of his teachings, I would have donned my best dinner jacket and bow tie and given it the old

Anton Du Beak (or whatever he's called). The fact is, the blind were being led. We didn't know how else to get into this mystical art.

Moving half way across the world wasn't an option for me at the time, so the VHS info was a goldmine of instruction. Of course, I now realise that a lot of what we were doing, was as much use as a chocolate fireguard. I am certainly not one of those Black belts who think that their system, and their system alone has all the answers. A broken jaw, an ear that was detached and several broken ribs later, I realised that there may well be an element of the 'Emperor's new clothes', about Gracie Jiujitsu. Don't misunderstand, I do believe that BJJ is a very good addition to a more holistic approach to self-defence. Does it have all the answers? No. Just like any system is not complete and able to deal with each, and every possible attack scenario.

Gi Or No Gi?

As time and tide have shifted, so too has the perception that the Gi is still the most relevant aspect of Brazilian Jiu-Jitsu. Now, some may argue (myself included), that only Gi training is actually Brazilian Jiu-Jitsu and everything else is Submission Wrestling. But it has to be said, this Submission Wrestling sure looks a lot like Brazilian Jiujitsu. If it quacks like a duck and walks like duck and all that?

Back in the day, there was a fierce rivalry between the Gi practitioners and the No Gi enthusiasts (Lutre Livre). The fallout manifested in many a straightener between the art's respective students and champions. One of the most notable encounters was between Rickson Gracie, Jiujitsu's answer to superman, and a gentleman by the name of Hugo Duarte, a well-known practitioner of Lutre Livre (free fighting). The Lutre Livre guys shunned the Gi and opted for a system that is more in line with today's No Gi game. There ensued a couple of anything goes fights between the two martial artists. The first and notable one occurred on Copa Cabana beach in beautiful Rio de Janeiro. It was a frenetic encounter that concluded with the legendary Rickson Gracie, mounted on Duarte and giving him a rather brutal, yet effective lesson in Gracie Jiujitsu (a good old fashioned bitch slapping). The second encounter, ended in much the same way. Now, does that answer an argument that training in the Gi is better than training without? Hell no. What it proves, is that on those given days Rickson was victorious. It was Rickson Gracie, the best of the best fighting. You could have put a prime Mike Tyson in front of him and my money would have been on Rickson Gracie.

My own perspective, and I honestly like training in both Gi and No Gi, is that they both have their place of importance in the modern-day grappling scenario.
Training in the Gi will make your defences really watertight. There are more material levers to pull, push and use to control an opponent.
I always remember the first time I rolled with a BJJ Blue belt. I had never, up to this point, met a bona fide BJJ practitioner. One day a guy walked into my gym and told me that he had trained in the USA under Pedro Saur, a Rickson Gracie representee and black belt. I was very impressed and of course I wanted to roll. My club at the time was more wrestling and MMA orientated. We didn't wear the Gi much, although I was a black belt in traditional jujitsu. Anyway, we begin to roll (No Gi), we went back and forth for maybe 10 to 15 minutes with no subs or real dominance from either of us. I was elated to have not only survived, but given as 'good as I got', with a BJJ Blue belt. This guy was a really nice bloke and invited me to his Gi session in a not too far town the following weekend. Of course I was going to go. The chance to learn BJJ from a Blue belt was

drawing me like iron filings to a magnate.

The following weekend I turned up at the gym where my new friend had his BJJ class. There was only the two of us (BJJ was still relatively unknown). The coach threw me a Gi top and a belt and said let's roll (nothing like easing me in then). The result of this roll was completely different to our first. I was being manhandled. Thrown about like a paper bag caught in a hurricane. I tapped more than I had ever done in all of my training up to that point. I literally felt like a baby having his candy taken by an adult. I was sold. I left the dojo that day with a mixture of slight embarrassment and excitement. I could live with the shame, at least my students hadn't bore witness to me getting my arse handed to me (ah ego, that most fickle of mistress). I just wanted to learn. I wanted to be the one making another human fly through the air with the ease that I had experienced. If this was BJJ, sign me up. I was all in. Of course, up until this point, I thought that I had been privy to BJJ's techniques via the Gracie VHS instructional series. But no amount of drilling these fundamentals could have prepared me for that first real roll with a BJJ blue belt.

Enter the wrestler

As the art gained worldwide momentum, there was a shift in the way that the art was represented. Competitions such as the ADCC, a No Gi competition that pitted the best of the best against each other for (what was then) a lucrative deal for the winners.

The ADCC gave rise to some of the arts legendary grapplers. People like Marcelo Garcia, Royler Gracie, Eddie Bravo et al, all used the competition to cement their position as the top No Gi competitors in the world.

It can be argued that No Gi is the 'all singing, all dancing' sexy relative of BJJ. For one it appears to be a faster and more dynamic art. By the time of the first ADCC, the general fan base of the art, were ready for a new approach to competition. For decades, the IBJJF had monopolised the BJJ competitive circuit. And although it was/is a prestigious event to win, there was a real need to look beyond Gi grappling and the tried and tested format that it had employed for many years.

In MMA, several behemoth wrestlers had entered the fray, and had been very successful in not only taking people down and utilising their number one tactic, ground and pound, to take the wins, but they were also very skilled in staying on their feet or regaining standing positions if needed. This obviously hindered the BJJ practitioners, who, it has to be said, didn't strike particularly well. Wrestling was also well represented at ADCC. The tide was turning and the importance of learning to wrestle was at its height.

In the UK, there were more No Gi competitions and brackets added to the standard fare on offer. Sub only comps started to be introduced to the usual Calander of events. This gave rise in the number of gyms that focused solely on the No Gi aspects of grappling.

The Wrestling heritage in the UK

What isn't generally known is that wrestling has a rich history in the United Kingdom. In the Lancashire mill and mining communities in times long gone, the workers would let off steam in the many Catch as catch can (catch) wrestling clubs. In the towns around Wigan and Manchester especially, the art was well represented. Legendary Catch wrestlers such as Billy Riley and Karl Gotch honed their skills in rundown sheds that had minimum matting and sparse facilities. These men were tough and supremely well-conditioned athletes. They trained fanatically in their art placing emphasis on aliveness and combat conditioning. The techniques that were apparent in the system, a combination of Greco roman wrestling and painful submission holds are a fair representation of todays no Gi system. The art of Catch is still very much alive and kicking in the North of England and indeed globally. The Catch Wrestlers are a very important part of our rich history. My experience of Catch Wrestlers is quite extensive as I have competed a lot in both Gi and no Gi competitions. A lot of these tournaments where in the North of England (catch territory).

The style of a good Catch Wrestler is or rather can be hard to deal with for someone from a pure BJJ background. I first encountered good Catch Wrestling at the old Defence Unlimited gym in Manchester. A guy that trained there *Ian Bromley, had the most gnarled ears I had ever seen up to that point. We used to have some great rolls, where I would usually get dominated by his hold downs and explosive style. Ian was a fantastic guy; he would share his techniques and was always happy to help in whatever I needed on the mats. Ian was the best on any given day on those mats, but as I have said, he wasn't cocky just a guy that loved to train. My respect for Catch is immense as a result of meeting people like Ian and *Jack Mountford, another ambassador for the art. Internationally, people like Kazushi Sakuraba, had notably beaten several members of the Gracie family using Catch Wrestling. Catch Wrestling was enjoying something of a revival after these notable wins.

*Both Ian and Jack have now passed away. They leave a rich legacy in their arts history.

The King Is Dead- Long Live The King!

When we talk about No Gi, we need to address the man that is considered the greatest of all time (GOAT). Stand up Mr Gordon Ryan. Ryan has earned a fierce reputation for his dominance at ADCC and other high-profile competitions. Known for his technical mastery and not unfounded confidence, Ryan is something of a marmite taste to many, you either love him or hate him. But one thing you can't argue with is his skill and unparalleled success in the no Gi domain.

Arguably, Ryan's rise to the pinnacle of this genre, has brought a lot of eyes to the sport, and helped its growth exponentially. No story of Ryan would be complete without his coach and mentor John Danaher being mentioned. Danaher, came from the legendary Renzo Gracie stable in New York city. His teaching methodology is akin to listening to Professor Steven Hawking explaining the universe. In short, the man exemplifies the 'theory into practice' model of learning.

It is obvious that Ryan would still be a phenom, even without Danaher's influence, but every team or athlete, needs an outside perspective in order to flourish and reach their potential. The Danaher/Ryan partnership seemed like the perfect blend. Danaher is credited with the introduction of the leg lock game, although it was Dean Lister who introduced Danaher to this concept. The leg lock system certainly exposed a lot of holes in people's games and understanding of the sport. Danaher, made the statement 'why ignore 50% of the human body' famous. But the question as to why leglocks were alien to most BJJ competitors is an interesting one.

Traditionally in the "old school' Jiujitsu gyms, leg locks (other than the straight ankle lock) were seen as a cheat move. Ludicrous when you consider Danaher's quote. But if we explore the rationale behind this feeling that leg locking is an unfair addition to the competitive game, then we should think in terms of the hierarchy of Jiujitsu

The Hierachy Of Jiu-Jitsu

In terms of Jiujitsu's order of importance in combat strategy and techniques, there are certain aspects and aims that usurp others (hierarchy). The ultimate goal is to take down, control and render an opponent helpless whilst taking minimum damage in the application of each aspect in achieving this aim. In a broader statement, the details are of paramount importance. An example of this would be in the emphasis that 'old school' jiujitsu places on the ability to pass the guard. In terms of guard playing, back in the day, the closed guards held more importance and relevance than they perhaps enjoy today. Therefore, foot locks were deemed to be a lazy option and seen as a 'cop out' for people not versed in guard passing tactics and principles. This thought process goes some way into explaining why leglocks were a neglected skill in jiujitsu's rich and varied history.

Danaher, the genius strategist, recognised that there was a gap in knowledge amongst most of his teams' rivals. Of course, he, and the likes of Gordon Ryan would capitalise. The watching fans, and importantly the Jiujitsu community quickly caught onto this concept of attacking the lower limbs.

For me, 99.9% old school, leglocks are not a massive part of my game, although I do see their importance. I also watch some of my younger students who, for want of a better term, are 'YouTube experts', who play the leg lock game fairly well. It is always interesting when I run a drill whereby the students have to pass the guard and hold the guard, using only sweeps. It is always the 'wannabe' leg lockers that struggle to pass the guard. I also have a couple of my black belts that have embraced the leg lock systems and are absolute nightmares to deal with.

Whatever your views are on this topic, Danaher was right we shouldn't 'neglect 50% of the human body', but that works both ways. Do the leglock systems, but don't ignore the upper limbs, the neck and the essential skill of guard passing.

I don't know where the future of Jiujitsu is heading, and whilst I hold with the philosophy that there really isn't 'anything new under the sun', there will always be innovation of the things we have done in the past.

Don't sleep on the art. Blink and there will be a new king on the throne. At the time of writing this book, Gordon Ryan has stepped away from competing due in the main to health issues. There will always be a prince in waiting. Someone in the wings ready to ascend to the highest of highs.

PART 3

THE DRUGS DON'T WORK, OR DO THEY?

"success is very much like a drug" - William B. Irvine

We now come to a much-debated aspect of Jiujitsu and competition, what part do performance enhancing drugs (PEDs) play in modern jiujitsu?
We have mentioned Gordon Ryan, and acknowledged his place in the modern jiujitsu world. Ryan makes no secret of the fact that he uses PEDs. He argues that the majority of modern-day athletes within combat sports are using some kind of performance enhancer.
What are PEDs and how do they enhance performance in sports like Jiujitsu and MMA? The most common and widely known PED is Anabolic steroids. These act as a synthetic version of testosterone and increase muscle mass, overall strength and importantly aid recovery rate. Undoubtably these benefits are what draw so many of the top athletes to use a PED.
The training alone to be a top-level competitor is brutal. Recovery is essential in order to just show up day in and day out and put their body through the amount of training that is required to reach the higher echelons of their chosen sport.
The downside of PED use is it can carry certain risks to health. Gordon Ryan has significant issues with his gut health and although it is not proven that PEDs have contributed to this issue,

those that are Ryan critics are quick to try and make a connection. There are certainly some real and worrying health issues that are apparent with prolonged use of steroids et al. These include Liver damage and heart disease. As of this present time there are no testing platforms within the grappling competitive circuit. It could be argued that given the risks and the fact that PEDs give some amazing advantages, that there should be regular testing in order to allow for fairness and a level competitive field.

Of course, there are many athletes that are natural and shun the use of PED use in order to compete. One of the biggest rivals to Gordon Ryan in recent years has been Nicky Rod, AKA the Natty King. The two, once training partners, have built a rivalry both on the mat and off, with Nick Rod calling out Gordon for his PED use. It is common knowledge that in all of their matches, Ryan has come out victorious. Ryan has levelled the criticism that Nicky Rod is also on PEDs, something that is vehemently denied. Rod actually went for testing and came back clean. In contrast to Ryan, Nick Rod is still active on the competitive circuit, recently winning the Craig Jones invitational and one million dollars in prize money.

Whatever your thoughts on PEDs, the truth is that you still require a modicum of talent and skill in order to make the best use of their given attributes. Gordon Ryan would still be an amazing competitor even if he had never taken a PED.

Playing Devil's advocate, I would still love to see a match between Ryan and Nicky Rod, given that Rod has made such incredible progress in his Jiujitsu since the last encounter.

In terms of PED use for Joe Average that is a matter for the individual. And, as long as the person taking PEDs knows the risks, then all good. Personally, I would be fearful of taking Anabolic steroids. I struggle to take a paracetamol if I have a headache so the thought of putting something in my body that potentially could lead to kidney or heart issues is abhorrent. Do I agree with their use in competition, absolutely not. I believe that a competition should be a fair exchange of technical skill between two people who are at the same weight, grade or experience etc. The added advantage of steroids is akin to taking a gun to a knife fight.

Let's not confuse this with jiujitsu's original mission statement.

Jiujitsu was developed to give the lighter, weaker person the advantage over a heavier, larger opponent. But and this is a big but, the advantage is in the skill vs no skill approach.

There has always been those that look for any advantage when it comes to sport. The use of PEDs is nothing new. Body builders have historically used Steroids in order to 'assist' their natural attributes. The use of PEDs in MMA was prevalent up until a few years ago when testing was introduced. I have people in my gym that are using testosterone therapy. The results they are getting is astounding. The dad bod has been replaced by a physique that looks like it is chiselled from marble. But as noted there are risks associated with this practice. It is advised that you get tested by a Dr to see if your testosterone levels are indicative of starting any kind of treatment.

As I have said, I am ok with having a 'dad bod'. If I was younger and felt that I needed some help in certain areas, I might be tempted, or at least seek advice from my Dr.

GARY SAVAGE

TRAINING SMART!

"I hated every minute of training, but I said 'Don't quit. Suffer now and live the rest of your life as a champion- Muhammad Ali

For longevity or for optimising your abilities without PEDs, there are things that you can do off the mats. My own training over the years has changed as I have got older, had injuries or as a result of motivational changes.

When I was young and (relatively) pain free, and competing in both MMA and Jiujitsu, my routine was very focused. On the mats, I drilled and rolled daily with one day a week taken as a recovery day. Below is my typical weeks training regimen.

Monday-Saturday * Rest Day Sunday *

Early morning distance run (5 miles), interspersed with sprint training. Afternoon/ early evening either Jiujitsu tech drilling and rolling, wrestling, Judo or striking (Boxing or Muay Thai). No matter the split, every day except rest days I would train Jiujitsu. Combat conditioning was also a part of my daily routine. I used the body weight exercises favoured by catch wrestlers, i.e. Hindu squats, Hindu push ups, sit-ups, plank holds and resistance training.

This routine was hard. By Sunday my body was physically broken and sore. In hindsight I neglected my nutritional needs and gave little importance to a good stretching program.

This was my routine for many years. I had the resting heart rate of an elite level athlete, felt strong and could roll for hours without too much stress on my body.

Back then I didn't have access to a personal trainer. I had a friend who was a long-distance runner, so I asked to train with him. He introduced me to good form when running and the importance of sprint and hill training to build stamina. I went from wheezing my way over a mile, to running a comfortable 5 miles before I went to my day job. I cannot stress enough the importance of good road work for any combat athlete. As I got older, I switched from road running to track, which helped take some strain off of my knees.

Hill climbs were my least favourite part of running, but I understood the importance. My distance running was always done with a sense of competition. I measured my progress against my long-distance running friend, always trying to keep up with him (I never did, but I got closer as time went on).

The training I did to get physically stronger was always done without using mechanical aids. Bodyweight and resistance training, that in some ways mimicked actual jiujitsu or wrestling moves, was always more interesting to me. If I am honest, going to a gym and lifting weights bored me, although time has mellowed my views, I now see the great benefits of adding a good weights program to any training regime.

I took inspiration from Karl Gotch, a legendary figure in the Catch Wrestling world. Gotch started his day performing up to 1,000 Hindu squats and press-ups. Now, in truth I never got to that level of intensity, but I did perform hundreds of these exercises every session. If you have never tried a Hindu squat or press-up, add them to your routine, they are a fantastic cardio and muscle building addition to any training program.

The other aspects of my training, boxing, Thai boxing and wrestling were all required for my MMA training. I was very selective in the coaches I had. It was important to me to learn each individual art to the best of my abilities. I was never going to be good enough in any of the arts to go pro, but I got to a good standard and found physical benefit in practicing each as a separate entity.

When I got to my 50's, I had some niggling pains in my hips. This got worse over time and led me to seeking professional advice. The scans on both hips showed bone on bone. My consultant said that he had rarely seen worse in someone of my age, and was specific in stating that it was most certainly a result of my past training and combat experience. The pain obviously hindered my training and as a result of enforced inactivity my weight ballooned, my resting heart rate got progressively worse and I had blood pressure issues for the first time in my life.

I was extremely fortunate in that I got both hips replaced by the time I was 60 years old. The road to recovery has been hard, but I am finally getting back into shape. The change has been unbelievable. I walk pain free, can run (albeit slowly) and importantly can train again.

It is clear that the old training routines, the hard sparring and rolling had contributed to my hip issues. But the lack of understanding of good nutrition, stretching and the importance of supplements was a significant factor. Today's athlete's take correct nutritional and supplement advice. They stretch and measure their vitals on a regular basis. The leaps made in knowledge as to correct training practices has been unbelievable over the past few years. We would be stupid to not take heed of the gains made over time. Even in our later years we can train properly and with less stress on our joints.

Incorporating Yoga or Pilate's into your routine for older grapplers is beneficial. Including reps with light weights is also advisable in later life. And if your knees find the idea of running about as appealing as you find going to a pool party at Michael Barrymore's gaff, try walking.

Whatever your goals in jiujitsu, an off-mat regime is advised. Eat clean, get regular exercise, stretch and if able get your road work and weight training in. But this is not at the expense of your jiujitsu training. Marcelo Garcia, arguably the best grappler of his generation when asked about weight training et al, said that he didn't do any of that, he just trains jiujitsu. Maybe there is something in that. Grappling is thought to be the hardest in terms of energy expanse. You get an all-body workout from a good competitive roll. And it is widely acknowledged by any one that ever rolled with Marcelo, how for a small person, his strength, grips and explosive ability was unlike any one else they had rolled with. Now maybe Marcelo is just athletically gifted. Who knows? But there must be something in his philosophy. Some of the strongest people I ever rolled with were people who didn't do weights, run or do anything other than their job or hobby. One of the strongest beginners in my gym was a young Farmer. He had the sort of strength that you might associate with a power lifter. His strength had been built up from years of manual labour. Must be something in the manure. Another notable person that had incredible strength was a guy that was involved in rock climbing. Obviously, his grip strength was something else, but his cardio was amazing, this lad sweated less than Prince Andrew (allegedly).

There might be something to gain from these examples. A supplementary 'hobby' like rock climbing may benefit your jiujitsu. Although having said that the idea of clawing my way up Ben Nevis is about as appealing as sitting through a Katie Price concert.

Training is subjective. People have their own ideas and philosophies. My only advice really, is to find a routine that you enjoy and train smart. There is little point in trying to bench press the building, only to injure your back and having to take time off the mats recovering.

THE DEVIL IS IN THE DETAIL!

"Effectiveness is doing the right things, while efficiency is doing things right"- Peter Drucker

Jiujitsu is a complex art. The details are an important aspect in determining a successful application of a given move or objective. Latterly, my focus has shifted towards getting things right. Finding the balance between effective and efficient.
We hear the term 'invisible jiujitsu' used frequently. We associate this terminology with Rickson Gracie and latterly Henry Akins. But what is this idea, and is it just a fancy way of saying 'doing things right? I believe it is more than just a throw away ideology. It is arguably the most important aspect in jiujitsu, and the bedrock of mastering the art. Rickson Gracie is perhaps the most notable figure in modern jiujitsu. His skill and knowledge are unrivalled. His technique is the thing of folklore. People who have rolled with him or competed against him have all said that he is on a different level in terms of his ability and deep understanding of jiujitsu. These people are not weekend hobbyist's, they are multiple time world champions. They tell of Rickson's ability to know exactly what they were planning and to have the perfect counter. It has been told that during a roll, Rickson can tell you the submission he is about to hit and further, he will count it down from 10 to 0 and catch the sub. What is it that makes Rickson so effective. Yes, he was born into the first family of Jiujitsu. He

had tutelage from both his father and cousin Rolls Gracie, and a stable full of Gracie killers to roll with on a daily basis. But I believe that Rickson's ability comes from a different place. He has an ability to really look at a given technique and like scientist analyse and break it down. Invisible Jiujitsu is a term that describes the hidden, or rather missed concepts that make a move efficient.

As my jiujitsu has evolved I have gotten more into looking past the outcome of a move, and rather look at the mechanics that get it to the point of application. I have said before, I don't believe that there is such a thing as a basic technique. Rather there are basic principles that when understood and applied will make any move more efficient. And, whilst there are (in my opinion) no basic techniques, there certainly are moves that are high percentage. These techniques are those that can be applied in a variety of positions. This makes them of importance when learning a technique. For example, an armbar can be applied from mount, side control, full closed, half and open guard and even the back mount positions. It therefore makes sense to focus on the minute details in order to make these high percentage moves efficient.

Attention to detail is paramount if you want your Jiu-Jitsu experience to be as full as possible. When you start Jiujitsu, you will be bombarded with a multitude of techniques. It can be very daunting and confusing. As you progress, you will start to build your game. You should have an understanding of the fundamental concepts and be able to make some of the technique's work in a live situation (rolling). I cannot stress enough; you should get good instruction. A coach who doesn't acknowledge your efforts, and when required, offer positive critique and guidance, is not a good fit for learning.

There needs to be a good balance in your early training phase between getting the knowledge and being 'taught' the mechanics and conceptual ideas that make a technique work.

At the start of my training, I was obsessed with the notion of leverage. The Gracie's espoused it as the core principle of their system. It was, to my mind, the factor that might separate BJJ from its relative combat systems. And, whilst the principle of leverage is an important one, I now believe it is a single piece of a jigsaw and that without creating the right angles and managing the distance properly, then leverage is and always will be an isolated jigsaw piece, that alone makes no sense and doesn't allow for the full picture to be viewed.

Concepts are the key to understanding jiujitsu. Gathering a shed load of techniques, without understanding how they function is like trying to swim in treacle (you can't move forward). Correct analysis and empirical research will serve you well in your quest to learn jiujitsu. In contrast, just understanding concept's without trying to make them applicable in live rounds is equally as lame. Theory needs practice in the same way that a fish needs water. A good BJJ coach will be able to answer any question that you might have around the fundamental concepts. A great BJJ coach will still be asking questions and seeking answers themselves.

Lets break down the key concepts that are apparent in jiujitsu.

Distance management

In any combat system, distance management is an important concept to grasp. Fighting at the correct range can be the difference between success and failure. In jiujitsu, distance management can apply to any aspect of the art, from guard passing to guard retention, controlling the distance is paramount to making the technique effective. An example of distance management in classical jiujitsu (Gracie JJ) would be in the way that the jiujitsu combatant might cover the distance to clinch against a striker. You can witness it in the early Royce era UFC's. Royce would have his left hand outstretched, his right fist to his jaw and he would stomp his lead leg to the opponent's knee. This would proceed him closing the distance and clinching before taking his opponent to the mat.

In sport jiujitsu the guard pass is a great example of having a good understanding of distance management. The ability to shut down your opponent's hip movement and neutralise their frames will assist in you guard passing attempt. And in direct contrast, the guard player needs to retain distance to allow their hips to move and create the necessary angles to sweep, attack, set frames and escape.

Connection

Connection is a term that is mostly associated with Rickson

Gracie. The key principle is that you create pressure that is far greater than just putting your weight on someone. Connection is a more complex idea that is created through utilising other core principles like distance management, angle use, leverage etc. You can really add pressure to a hold down by connecting your hips, controlling your opponent's shoulders and disrupting their spinal alignment. Connection is a difficult principle to explain, but easy to show. Poor connection will lead to sloppy technique, bad control and submission attempts that are easy to counter. Look up Henry Akins (Rickson Gracie Black belt) for some great details on connection. Even better, if you ever get the chance to train with Rickson, take it.

Rickson's seminars are said to be legendary. He often asks the black belts in attendance to demonstrate a technique such as the mount. He then proceeds to escape with relative ease and shows the blackbelt the technique done with correct application. It can be a subtle difference, but will make all of the difference. This is true connection. The meeting of the physical with other aspects, such as correct breathing, angles and distance awareness. People talk about feeling black belt pressure. But this is just an example of connection and can be taught to anyone and at any grade.

Remember, there are no basic techniques, just basic principles that make the techniques work.

Angles

Angles are the missing piece in the whole leverage mystery. For decades, jiujitsu students have chased this idea that the moves are effective because of the use of leverage. Yes, it is true, however, without creating the right angle you can't apply a lever.

It was around brown belt that I started to place emphasis on this concept of angles. I struggled, like most, to comprehend the Gracie tenant of leverage. Yes, I could make a move work in rolling, but I never really had the principle in my head. I was just doing what I had observed. It was something considered a very easy move (remember there are no basics), the scissor sweep, that helped with my understanding. I was hitting it occasionally, but often times couldn't make it work when my opponent was expecting it. It was a lightbulb moment when I broke down the move and utilised angles, correct distance management and connection to it. The move itself is almost impossible to do without creating the correct angle. But that in itself won't work without an understanding of body mechanics. If your opponent is sitting back on their heels, you require a lever. Your lever is in the pulling action to make them take their weight from their heels. Pull them forward and you only have to initiate enough momentum to sweep the lower half of their body, i.e. disrupt their connection. Now, without moving your hips, setting up your frame, positioning your body onto your hip, you won't be able to move them. Everything works together. Principles are like body parts, alone they look efficient, but they function when connected. The principal theory is the brain that brings everything together.

Breathing

Sounds crazy, we all breathe, but the use of correct breathing in jiujitsu will pay dividends to your technical ability. It is often overwhelming for beginners to be underneath someone applying correct pressure. They panic, make wild and reckless moves that ultimately lead to their downfall. Some even tap to the pressure, unable to breathe they just want the misery to end. Correct breathing is essential in making sure you are relaxed enough to move well, deal with bad positions and think of a strategy to escape. The act of slowing your breathing will in turn slow your heart rate and give you the energy that is required to use explosive movements. In turn correct breathing will add pressure to your hold down and allow you to continue past the point of physical fatigue.

Grip fighting

Grip fighting whether in the Gi or not, is an important skill/concept to grasp (pun intended). In the Gi, grip control can mean the difference in breaking balance for throws, controlling hold downs and securing submission attempts. No Gi grips are in the main for the same purpose but can be harder to achieve without the cloth to grip.

Grip fighting goes hand in hand with the other core concepts such as distance management and connection. Developing grips is a tough process and can lead to that mostly unknown condition 'Cauliflower fingers". Be careful with your grips. Don't employ a Vulcan death grip every time you take the Gi. Rather keep you grip relaxed until you feel a reaction or are ready to use some force to move your opponent. In no Gi, you should concentrate on developing your essential skills such as the Greco Roman holds, underhooks and double under's.

Leverage

Once we are fully appraised of the other core concepts, we can achieve the Nirvana of BJJ, leverage.

As stated earlier, the Gracie family built an empire on this concept. Their mantra being 'we didn't invent the wheel, rather we introduced the jack that can lift the car and change the wheel' (paraphrase). In other words, leverage. It was the secret sauce that attracted the smaller, weaker individual who wanted to defend themselves. It was the equivalent of the old Charles Atlas advert were the weak guy gets sand kicked in his face and his girlfriend goes off with the meathead sand kicker as a result. Following a bit of training by Charles Atlas, our hero returns shredded and takes his revenge on the beach bully, and his girlfriend back in the process. Personally, he would have been better kicking the girlfriend to the curb long before the sand in the face confrontation, she sounds like a right one. Anyhow, I digress, the hero in the Gracie narrative is trained in jiujitsu and therefore doesn't need the muscle bod in order to win the day.

Leverage is a very important aspect. But as we have established, isn't as useful without creating the correct angles etc.

whether you are at the point in your training whereby you are starting to see these concepts in jiujitsu, or you are just copying the techniques parrot fashion, is not as important as you just getting started in the art. In time you will see beyond the end result of a technique and look into how and why it works.

This is what makes jiujitsu a lifelong endeavour. An understanding of concepts will serve you well into later life when your body isn't as capable of using strength or explosiveness. You will always be able to use angles, levers etc.

THE ART OF TEACHING!

"I have never let my schooling get in the way of my education'- Mark Twain

What about teaching jiujitsu as a career?

 I have taught Jiujitsu and martial arts in general for the best part of 30 years (almost half my life). When I started it wasn't really a viable profession. We taught out of old (drafty) village halls, sport centres and anywhere that we could just to follow our dreams. There wasn't really much money in teaching back in the day. We couldn't really charge a premium for our time, and there was always a lot of competition for student's. When BJJ first started gaining momentum, you would be surprised to learn that classes were still not busting at the seams with people wanting to learn. It was a slow and steady build. I recall starting an MMA class in a sports centre in Lancaster. I had put flyers out and posters etc. I am not sure what I expected, but it wasn't the reality of turning up each Saturday, only to twiddle my thumbs waiting for the influx of students to magically appear. This was the reality for a good few weeks, until, one fine Saturday, a gentleman called Nigel wandered in to my room. At first, I thought he had taken a wrong turn and was looking for the badminton courts. But no, Nigel (God bless him) was wanting to learn MMA. For a good few weeks, it was just me and Nigel. I taught him to punch, kick and grapple as best

I could. As time went on, we had another couple of people join. All good and tough lads that wanted to learn. Eventually we were in a position whereby we had to put on extra sessions to accommodate the interest we were accruing. I was never going to get rich from teaching out of a room in a sports centre but it was a great way to learn the ropes, to cut your teeth if you will. I learned how to teach. That seems like a glib statement, but it is one thing knowing, it is another showing. It became apparent to me quite early on that people learn at different paces and in different ways. Some learn through watching; other's more through listening and some by doing. Prior to setting up this MMA club, I had taught Japanese jujitsu and Karate. My biggest learning curve was when I was tasked with teaching the kids class. To say it was like herding cats is an understatement. Keeping an energetic 5-year old's attention is enough to cause a nervous breakdown. I realised that you have to be creative in holding a child's attention. The use of games and rewards like trophies for best student (good old fashioned bribery) seemed to work. I wouldn't like to go back to teaching kids, but in terms of serving an apprenticeship, it was invaluable. I always encourage my new coaches to start as kids class instructors. It teaches you how to engage, how to effectively communicate and how your technique has to be on the money.

As time went on, I have really honed my skills as a teacher. It is not enough to just demonstrate a technique. You have to engage people. Make them understand the nuance's and importantly encourage their efforts.

I once asked another coach what his teaching philosophy was. Without hesitation he said 'Fear. People learn best when they are scared'. I told him I disagreed with this and in fact, thought it a counterproductive way to teach. People close up when afraid. If you replace shouting and belittling with encouragement you will get a lot further in your quest to impart good jiujitsu. It kind of explains why some academies are full and others are barely ticking over. My academy has always had a friendly vibe. We laugh and joke, but train hard. People should enjoy attending a class, not be in fear of their life. Gyms that teach combat arts carry a bad reputation as it is, so why not try and break that idea and offer a warm and friendly atmosphere. Yes, it is not a knitting circle people are joining, it's a combat art. There will be pain and sweat. But that doesn't mean it has to be a nightmare inducing experience every time you pull up to the carpark. A gym will have a multitude of personalities, just pray that they don't all belong to the head coach. There is nothing worse than a coach who changes like the wind. We can all have off days, but at least consider how your moods might affect the students. A good gym will often have good facilities, be clean and a respectful place to train. This is all made possible by the coach. If you are training in a place that makes the original Daisy Fresh gym look like Bannatyne's, then consider whether it is at least clean and has top level coaching. The decor doesn't determine the quality of training, but it should at least be hygienic. If you are considering changing your day job to pursue a coaching position at least weigh up all of the issues that might arise. Often times people find a relatively cheap place to teach out of, but they don't factor in variables such as insurance, business rates, tax liability etc. You also need to get your charging criteria right. Don't always assume that just because you undercut your competition that you will be more successful. I have always charged a fair price. That doesn't mean cheap. It means that I know my worth and charge accordingly. People will pay more for quality. We use a combination of pay as you train and monthly inclusive packages. It works just fine. I have tried using these billing companies that promise you the earth but rarely deliver. It is easy enough to set up your own systems. My next tip is to get a good front of house manager. Someone who is there to take payment's, upsell your merchandise and generally be on hand to answer any questions from passing trade. We were blessed with our manager, John Boswell. He was almost like a partner in the gym rather than a manager. He sorted out all of our orders, kept records of attendance and generally came up with some fantastic marketing idea's. Sadly, last month John died. To say he left a massive hole in our lives is an understatement and is the reason I have dedicated this book to him. Get good people around you. It will make your life so much the easier.

Structure of classes is something I have tried and changed many times over the years. Today I rarely advocate classes that are longer than an hour (although I do have a couple of classes that run over an hour for different reasons). Kids classes are 45 minutes long (it is enough believe me). I have always advocated a good warm up followed by a stretching routine (maybe it should be the other way around). The next typical aspect will be a pass the guard hold the guard drill (no submissions only sweep and passing). This will often help me to decide what I am going to teach in the class (I rarely plan). The technique section will be no more than 4 related moves. We will look at the technique and its variables in situations where the move fails or is countered. The last part is the live training (rolling). This can be free rolling or positional/situational sparring. We mainly start on knees, although sometimes (space permitting) we start standing. I tend to teach a separate takedowns class. There are plenty of good Judo clubs in the area, so my classes are more wrestling based in approach.

However you teach your classes, there needs to be a good balance between drilling and aliveness. Showing a flashy move that you know has about as much validity as, oh I don't know, a multi-millionaire paying thousands of pounds to get a black belt in less than 4 years, it is not in the best interest of the student. There is a danger that our art will become as pantomime as some of the other arts that have become watered down over the years. When money overrides integrity and the moves become so ridiculous just to attract students that know no better, we are in trouble. Teaching is a very rewarding career. But, unless your second name is Gracie or you have won multiple World championships you might not get rich in monetary terms. You can however, be a rich person in terms of your life having meaning. Doing something you love, reaching people, enriching lives etc is always a good thing. You can make a decent living and you defo shouldn't listen to me saying you can't make a million pounds (you may).

I have never regretted one day of teaching or making teaching jiujitsu my main source of income. I have been blessed to meet some beautiful people, have some incredible moments and learn some in valuable lessons. I will teach until my light goes out. It was always my childhood dream to be a martial arts coach and I have achieved my goal. When I used to work the doors, I would regularly have (drunken) people come up and say 'do you remember me, you taught me jiujitsu when I was younger". I would always politely say 'of course, how the heck are you"? Usually when I asked if they were coming back, they would say 'yes'. Very rarely did I see them, other than the next week on the doors.

We, as coaches have an opportunity to impact people's lives. These students may not continue with the art (it is not for everyone), but you can be sure that your teaching and time will mean something in their story. The bars and nightclubs are full of blue belts who quit. Maybe this is the Bermuda Triangle for blue belts, they are to be found propping up a bar, telling anyone who will listen how they could put anyone to sleep without breaking a sweat. Don't be that guy. Continue training. Keep showing up until you can't physically do so anymore.

There is no magic formula other than, keep on keeping on. Whether you are a student, coach or maybe you are a regular person thinking about taking up this great art then just know that your life will be enriched by jiujitsu. Forget the slight downsides, the niggling pains, cauliflower ears and fingers, hips and knees that require medical attention, just 'belt up'. Or as Churchill advised, 'If you are going through Hell, keep going'.

FIND A JOB YOU LOVE AND YOU WILL NEVER WORK A DAY IN YOUR LIFE!

Long chapter title, but it is an important statement that requires some retrospect.

The good, the bad and the ugly.

As I have stated, I love teaching, Jiujitsu is my passion, my dream job. But and this is the point of this chapter, when your passion becomes your job, your sole source of making a living, paying your bills and feeding mouths etc, something changes. It has to. At the moment, perhaps you are in that period just before you get obsessed (not making the thumb and little finger surfy sign on all photo's), or maybe that particular boat has sailed and all you can think of is the Arte Suave. Great, enjoy. But when you cross over from student to teacher and or, owner of an academy, that feeling of complete freedom and loving just being 'in' the art will change. You have to follow a strict regime of teaching classes, giving 121 lessons, doing admin, making sure people are paid and keeping the lights on for another month. You will have less time to just enjoy your training. It is time to wear your big boy pants and become a responsible adult (shock and horror). It is not that you will lose your love for jiujitsu, but it's sheen will diminish slightly by the very fact that it has now become 'a job'. When you are the student, you can pick and choose your training regime. And although it is likely you will train as much as you can, the fact is you have that option. When you are a gym owner/coach this choice is somewhat made for you. Obviously, I am not saying that my experiences are the same for everyone, but I can say that there are days where I feel as if I am going to my job, rather than my passion. This is natural. After doing a 6–7-hour day of teaching, your body is physically broken. The thought that you have to get up out of a lovely warm bed at 6.00am to repeat the process the following day is sometimes not a pleasant one. Of course, I love the training, teaching and the people that I meet, but if anything is going to de-rail your enthusiasm, it is teaching a lot and not knowing how to switch off. For me, I have had times when I have lost my mojo. Resented the fact that I have to leave the comfort of my house, miss family gatherings or other experiences, because I am scheduled to teach in order to make money. The way I have got past these times of lethargy and resentment is to reflect on my life before I became a full-time coach. I have literally done some horrid jobs. Depressing, mind numbing activities that suck the very soul out of you.

I also have other interests away from my Jiujitsu and martial arts. I play guitar and love music. This is a great way to 'separate' your life, from work mode to having a hobby. Something that is as far removed from the job of teaching jiujitsu is healthy. Although, I do believe there are a lot of parallels between Jiujitsu and music. Both are artistic endeavours that require dedication and perseverance. But there is a clear definition. I know that jiujitsu is my job and I am so lucky that I am able to do it for a living. Whether I totally believe the statement that if you find something you love, you will never work a day in your life, is debateable. It is hard work to teach day in and day out. It becomes like anything in life, you can become jaded. This is where being creative and focused on continued learning and development will help you to reignite your passion for teaching. Recently my focus in my jiujitsu has returned to my original reason for taking up the art, self-defence. I am enthused by developing this area of my curriculum. The key is to keep things fresh. Jiujitsu is such a complex art that really you can always find areas of interest.

Anyway, enough of my ramblings. If you are considering Jiujitsu as a profession, just be aware that it is hard work and at times frustrating. It is also a most rewarding and exciting job. Think of it this way, you could be Prince Andrew's public relations officer. Give me that 6.00am 121 lesson on a cold February morning any day. OSSU

CONFESSIONS OF AN ADDICT

'They tried to make me go to rehab, I said no, no,no' Amy Winehouse

Jiujitsu will undoubtably enhance your life. More so, you will learn some valuable things that will help you in all aspects of your life.

For me, jiujitsu is my life's work. It is something I have invested hours, days, weeks and years in the pursuit of knowledge and understanding. It is, and will always be my reason for being. It is why at 61 years old I still get enthused at seeing the power that this great art has in changing lives. It doesn't matter where or when you start. What matters is you have started. It doesn't matter your background or back story; it will still treat you as an equal amongst its legions of followers. Whatever your reason/s are for taking up jiujitsu, be sure that you won't regret it. People outside of the art can never fully understand it. I have lost count of the times people have looked at me as if I am mad (they are right) when I have turned up to family gatherings with injuries. They may even pity me, which is ironic, as I pity them for their choice not to get involved in jiujitsu.

The fact is that jiujitsu will give more than it takes. It will teach you more than an Oxford degree course, if you choose to open your mind and observe what it has to offer. It is reflected in that old adage, 'you need to scratch below the surface, in order to find the truth'. There is a 'diamond in the rough', 'there's gold in them their hills', but you have to do the digging, the searching and have the tenacity to keep looking even when every stone appears to have been turned.

You will meet with inner conflict and self-doubt along the way, no one said it was going to be easy, but you can, and will reap the rewards, if you stay the course. If what you are doing isn't working for you, change your approach. The definition of madness is to keep doing the same things and expecting a different result. It is trial and error, a series of fails, before that breakthrough, eureka moment appears. There are no short cuts, as I have said throughout this book. Hard work, diligence and sacrifice will pay off. Quitting is never going to pay you back for the wasted hours. I am not sure what would define me had it not been jiujitsu and being a martial artist. I don't think I could just be one of those people that work a job they despise and live for the weekend. I am by my very nature an addictive person. Maybe had it not been jiujitsu I would be addicted to drink or drugs, or God forbid, train spotting. I do believe that the people that achieve a BJJ black belt are to a degree similar people. I had a great conversation with one of my black belts, Sam, not so long ago. Our lives although different shared some commonalities. We both had this addictive personality. I have seen it in the people I have trained over the years. I am not saying you have to be an addictive person to achieve a Black belt, but I do think it is something that is prevalent amongst those that do.

Addiction is a word that is associated with illness, bad things, poor life choices etc. But addiction to sports, fitness or any kind of educational goal can't be bad, can it?

As I have said earlier, in my youth I sacrificed a lot to pursue Jiujitsu. Relationships and most aspects of life took a back seat in my drive to achieving my goals. In this respect, addiction to anything is unhealthy. For me I don't have regrets. I look back only to remind myself that I was there. I am firmly of the view that we shouldn't beat ourselves up for our mistakes. They are merely learning opportunities. The real tragedy in life is to not live each and every day. We should try to make the present day better than the last, and above all, to strive to be our absolute best version.

The Man in the Mirror

I met an old man in a bar a few years ago. It turned out he was a high-ranking jujitsu dan grade. He had given his life to his art, built a good following and taught hundreds of people over the years. Yet, here he was, alone, looking into his beer glass as if it were a crystal ball, showing the many roads, he had walked. He came to life when we spoke about jujitsu and martial arts. It was as if the weight of the past 80 years fell from him, his soul burst into life and a fire reignited in his eyes. Briefly he was that young man, pursuing his passion. Living the memories as if he were transported back. His life was full and the blood flowed through his veins as he spoke. He showed me some very painful wristlocks and regaled me with stories of his travels teaching and learning. He had trained in Japan, China and made great memories and friendships along the way.

He had no wife, no family and was living on a barge, alone. His body was too frail to train anymore, but his mind was razor sharp. I left his company feeling richer for meeting him and yet sad. I am not completely sure if my sadness was for him or me. I know that one day I could be that old man looking into a glass searching for my past glory. Alone except for the memories that stay buried until someone digs them up in conversation. It was obvious that this man was an addict and that this was the price of his addiction. I asked him as I left his company if he could change anything in his life what would it be? His answer came without hesitation. 'Nothing, I would do it all again in a heartbeat'.

And if you asked the same question of me, my answer would be the same.

.

CONCLUSION

'It is better to live one day as a lion, than a lifetime as a sheep'!

Thanks for reading the ramblings of an old timer. I started this book as a way of just journaling my time in jiujitsu. I hope that you have found something herein that may benefit you or at least resonate. It has been a gift to share some of my experiences with you.

Thanks to all of my teachers over the years, especially Mario Sukata, the man who taught me the jiujitsu alphabet and so much more. Thanks also to my students and team of coaches at Savage MMA, you keep me young at heart. Special thanks to my business partner Hazel, we created something special. And last but certainly not least, thank you Grand masters Carlos and Helio Gracie for giving us the gift that keeps on giving, Jiujitsu.

If you have enjoyed this book and want to read more you can check out my other books "All aboard the Gracie Train' and "Does Karate work in a phone box", available on Amazon platforms.

Printed in Dunstable, United Kingdom